Open for
Interpretation

Open for Interpretation

A Doctor's Journey
into Astrology

Alicia Blando, MD

She Writes Press

Published 2023
Printed in the United States of America
Print ISBN: 978-1-64742-470-1
E-ISBN: 978-1-64742-471-8
Library of Congress Control Number: 2022918285

For information, address:
She Writes Press
1569 Solano Ave #546
Berkeley, CA 94707

Interior Design by Tabitha Lahr
Image on page 51 is courtesy of Science History Images / Alamy Stock Photo

She Writes Press is a division of SparkPoint Studio, LLC.

For all my teachers, especially my patients,
who have allowed me to learn from them.

For my parents and siblings,
who give me love and support.

Contents

Author's Note

To write this book, I relied upon my personal notes, travel logs, and researched facts when I could, and called upon my memory of these events and times of my life. I have changed the names of most but not all of the individuals in this book, and in some cases, I also modified identifying details in order to preserve anonymity. I occasionally omitted people and events, but only when that omission had no impact on either the veracity or the substance of the story.

There is a seeming contradiction in my chart. I first describe my sun sign as Gemini, and thereafter describe my sun as Taurus (being in the ninth house). This change reflects my evolution from studying Western (tropical) to Eastern (sidereal or Vedic) astrology. No matter which system is used, the astrology interpretation can still describe the same person. Please see my explanation on pages 180–181.

Chapter 1:

A Professional Student

The idea for the pursuit of a rule book for life had started in 1990 during my medical training in New York City. The intensity of the clinical experiences and the need to learn extensive amounts of information brought about an emotional roller coaster of anxiety and self-doubt, mixed with a competitive spirit. I feared failure. I questioned whether I would become a doctor. The city offered opportunities to get readings from tarot card readers, mediums, astrologers, and psychics. New York City was where I started asking these practitioners for advice. I'd gotten straightforward readings as well as vague answers that I was on the right path. In the end, I finished my training by taking one day at a time and overcoming each challenge to the best of my ability.

My curiosity about the divination arts continued even as I worked to establish a medical practice. I'd met some genuine soothsayers and was interested in what they saw in my future. Eventually, I became more absorbed in how they got their information. I focused on astrology because I liked that the subject grew from the science of astronomy. If I could learn how these prognosticators got information about a client's circumstances, I might have a clue about a guidebook for life.

When I decided to go into the medical field, I knew, in general terms, what doctors did. They helped people who were sick. I learned basic terminology, function, and interaction of the body systems. I applied myself to the study of medicine and learned the process of becoming a physician.

Like medical school, astrology had fundamental rules, which meant it could be learned. Interpretation and prediction followed guidelines. After medical training, studying how the movement and position of celestial objects influenced man and nature was made pleasant because I didn't have to rely on this knowledge for an occupation.

So here I was seven years later in 1997, in my midthirties, on a beautiful Saturday morning in Miami waiting for an astrology class to start. I'd heard about Iris, the instructor, from a friend. About six months earlier, I'd attended a Wednesday night demonstration of her psychic and astrological abilities with some friends. She'd told me that being a doctor was in line with my ninth house of higher education. I was excited to learn that she offered astrology classes because I wanted to find out more about what she referred to as *houses*, and why she told me that I would do long-distance traveling in the future. I'd always dreamed about traveling. I could find out more about her process, and it didn't interfere with my job as a physician.

My internal alarm clock woke me at 4:30 a.m., a habit from medical training. I arrived in the North Miami classroom by 8 a.m. Class didn't start for another hour, but I brought coffee and would look at some notes I'd taken during the couple of astrology classes I'd already attended.

Slowly, the other students trickled into the modular office trailer and picked their seats. My preference in classroom settings was to sit in the back close to the entrance so as not to disturb people if I wanted to take a break or just leave, but Étienne, Iris's assistant, always had us move our chairs in a semicircle so that we all would be facing our teacher and the dry-erase board by her right side. The small space fit the usual group of thirteen to fifteen students comfortably. There were only one or two faces I'd recognized from the past two classes I'd attended. Iris held classes intermittently, so there was no formal curriculum or continuity.

Étienne had a bright personality to match her red hair. She looked to be around my age.

After greeting the class, she sat by the window collecting our birth data; she looked up the positions of the planets at the time, date, and location of our births in a thick, red paperback titled, *The American Ephemeris for the 20th Century: 1900 to 2000 at Midnight.* She handed each of us our information and then showed us how to plot the planets in the construction of our astrological charts, saying, "You're going to need this for the workshop."

I kept my list from prior classes inserted in my notebook. I flipped through the pages to find the chart I had drawn. It was a circle divided into twelve sections, or houses, that were assigned a constellation according to my time of birth. Each house represented a different area of life. Each of the nine planets was positioned in the sign (constellation) where it was located at the time of my birth.

1. *Self, Appearance, Health*
2. *Speech, Food & Drink, Finances*
3. *Siblings, Short Trips, Art, Communication*
4. *Mother, Home, Education, Vehicles, Ancestors*
5. *Romance, Children, Intellect, Intuition*
6. *Health, Disease, Enemies, Debt, Litigation, Labor*
7. *Partner, Public, Moral Conduct*
8. *Sex, Death, Longevity, Legacy, Accidents, Scandal*
9. *Higher Education, Teachers, Luck, Spirituality, Foreign Voyages*
10. *Reputation, Public Image, Government, Commerce*
11. *Hopes, Wishes, Dreams, Income, Social Clubs*
12. *Institutions, Isolation, Secrets, Expenditures, Losses, Bed Comforts, Foreign Voyages*

The natural horoscopic chart with
common significations of each house.

Étienne had been the greeter at the Wednesday night demonstration six months ago. And like that night, after giving attendees their birth chart, she stayed in the background. She only got up if Iris instructed her to write on the dry-erase board.

Once Iris arrived, she took a seat in the front of the class and, for the most part, stayed seated while lecturing in her strong New York accent. Iris looked to be in her late sixties to early seventies with black hair and her signature dark clothing. All the students, including myself, started taking notes once she started speaking.

In this class, she stressed that timing was important. The time of birth was just as important as the date and location of birth. A more focused description of the person could be obtained the more accurate the birth data. This statement stuck in my mind because the exact time of birth wasn't always known; the mother and doctor could approximate the time, which could be recorded differently on the birth certificate.

"You ever notice some twins that are totally different?" she asked. "They're born on the same day but not at the same time."

Twins, especially identical, were a great example, because identical twins come from the same fertilized egg and it was thought that their DNA, their genetic material, was also identical. Experiments have been done on twins to determine the effect of their environment on certain traits like height, weight, intelligence, and behavior, with the belief that environment was the only influencing variable.

But according to recent research, identical twins only share almost identical (not duplicate) genetic material, thus accounting for different personality traits, however subtle, even with the same environmental influences. Could different birth times, even by a minute, be another means to explain the variation? This consideration was interesting; twins, if raised in the same environment, could be used in experiments to answer astrological as well as medical questions since they had a built-in control system with almost identical DNA.

My chart described that on the day of my birth, the Sun was in the constellation of Gemini, meaning that the Sun had the constellation of Gemini in the background. To the east, the group of stars rising above the horizon was the constellation of Virgo. This made me a Gemini with Virgo rising. Astrologers believe these astronomical descriptions can define us, and the organization of the planets in a horoscope represents a blueprint of our lives.

From the date, time, and location of birth, this blueprint of our lives can give information on twelve areas of our life, including a description of self, how we deal with family members, our finances, and how we express ourselves. The placement of planets on a horoscopic diagram can even describe predisposition for certain occupations and diseases. As such, how was this subject never a part of medical training? It would be a great tool for preventative health consultation as an adjunct to any medical protocol.

I scrutinized my horoscope for clues as to when and how I got more interested in deciphering astrological charts than EKGs and X-rays. Fear came to mind. During medical training, I strived to do my best for patients, but there was the underlying fear—fear of making mistakes and not being good enough.

Bronx, New York, 1991

I longed to be a god.

As I hurried through the halls of the Bronx County Hospital to take care of a medical emergency, a recurring dream came to mind. In the dream I was in a cold sweat, running, running through passageways as fast as I could. Heart pounding.

This Thursday night, rushing through these dark corridors felt like déjà vu, and was made bleaker by the thought of decisions I had to make in the next hour.

There was always a lull in the evenings, after patients got

their dinner, took their evening meds, and settled down for bed. The floor busied again during the change of shifts that occurred between 11 p.m. and 2 a.m. As the outgoing and incoming nursing staff made their rounds, they eyeballed their charges and discussed what needed to be done in the next eight to twelve hours.

When on call, my senses were always on high alert all the way to 5 or 6 a.m.—the homestretch of my twenty-four-hour shift. I used to take pride when called "Doctor." These days, every time I heard the word, my body tightened and then loosened with an irritated sigh, and I thought, *What now?* Everyone who talked to the physician on night duty needed something to be done: scut work, detailed tasks like checking radiology reports, and drawing blood took a lot of time but had to be done—quickly, to save energy for unexpected emergencies. A quiet night was rare.

I never got used to the stress and chaos in the hospital. I just kept my head down and did my job. Time couldn't be wasted complaining. There was too much to do.

Some on-call doctors learned to sleep at the drop of a hat. Not me. I hardly slept. They woke with only the blare of the beeper. I just lay there, waiting for the inevitable series of shrill beeps, followed by a voice coming from the plastic box. We placed the beeper next to our ears, dialed to the loudest setting. No matter how deep asleep or how fatigued we might have been, the jarring effect jump-started our hearts and prepared us for action. The piercing voice of the operator would anchor the location of the emergency in our memory.

During the occasional downtime, the doctors on night duty spent time in the call room located in a separate building from the hospital, connected by corridors. The space was similar to a military barracks with six beds. Coed. No privacy. But we never lounged for long. I got plenty of exercise when working.

Tonight, the code, the crisis, was on my assigned wing, 5E, room 516. Racing up the stairwell of the main building from the second-floor on-call room was faster than waiting for the elevators. It gave me time to ponder. Who was in room 516? Was it the emaciated kid who got the human immunodeficiency virus (HIV) along with herpes? Or was it the thirty-two-year-old woman, HIV positive with pneumonia? Only three years older than me. She injected heroin.

Would my efforts help them survive?

Charging into the room, I barked, "Vitals." It was the woman with pneumonia. I squeezed around the crash cart to the head of the bed. It had been pulled away from the wall, making room for me.

The head nurse, used to the routine, calmly declared, "BP, 50 over palp, unresponsive." She would inform us whether our actions would have any effect.

Looking down, I saw that the patient's face was so gaunt that she looked like a skull with hair. The partially closed eyelids showed only the whites of her eyes. There was no more struggling for breath, no more pain. She was gone.

"How long? What does she have running? Any advanced directives?" I asked.

"Earlier, she was able to eat some of her dinner. Normal saline, wide open. No."

"Damn," I muttered under my breath, now wide-awake. Full code! In record time, I double-gloved, gowned, and donned a mask. What was I doing here? She was already gone.

"Showtime, Doctor," the respiratory therapist commented as he handed me an endotracheal tube.

While securing the artificial airway to the patient's lungs, all I could hear was my own breathing. Moisture was building against my mask. For the next ten minutes, I played God, trying to breathe life back into a body that had already surrendered.

From my vantage point, I surveyed the situation. The curtain partition was drawn as if it could shield the roommate from all the commotion we'd just made in this tight space. In our haste, wrappers, syringes, and medication containers were strewn all over the bed and floor. I met the nurse's expectant stare and answered, "Time of expiration: 2:21 a.m." That was the information she needed to fill out her forms.

The patient's features had been eerie before we started, but now they were grotesque, with her chin cocked up and a tube protruding from the side of her mouth. I was disgusted at what we'd put this woman through.

Do no harm.

We'd pounded, pushed fluids, and tried to revive this person. Back to what? She wasn't going to get better. I was glad that she'd passed quickly. Putting her on a ventilator would've prolonged her torture and delayed her dying. She was in the unit less than two weeks.

Primary diagnosis: cardiorespiratory failure due to *Pneumocystis carinii* pneumonia. Secondary diagnosis: HIV infection.

No family members were listed in the chart, so no one to call. Not unusual.

In 1991, four years after I'd first heard about HIV, scientists were still trying to understand how it worked and medical providers were attempting to control it. Although associated with the gay community, HIV could be transmitted with any exchange of tainted blood or body fluids. IV drug users, legal or illegal, who shared needles; anyone, straight or gay, who did not practice "safe sex"; *and* health-care workers were all at risk for the disease. Patients with HIV eventually progressed to end-stage AIDS (acquired immunodeficiency syndrome). The virus attacked all body systems—the lungs, the heart, the brain—until they stopped normal functioning. Even skin developed cancer. I learned to expect multisystem organ failure when answering emergency calls to almost any room in this hospital.

With the death certificate completed, I walked through the gloomy corridors, down the stairwell, and headed toward the call room, hoping the rest of the night would be uneventful. It had been nonstop activity all day.

I realized that the oath to *do no harm* was not a promise but only a hope with good intentions.

I was no god.

Earlier in the afternoon on this same Thursday, the infectious disease physician's assistant, PA Hilde, cornered me as she made her rounds. "Doctor, there are three lumbar punctures that need to be done. The recommendations were made last week." She needed body fluid, specifically cerebrospinal fluid (CSF).

CSF is what bathes and nourishes the brain and spinal cord. Analysis of the contents helped in the diagnosis and treatment of many neurologic disorders. The information, along with other laboratory data, was compiled and analyzed to establish treatment protocols for HIV. Hospitals became human research laboratories, with the medical staff as technicians.

"I just got on the floor. I'll see what I can do." My to-do list was already lengthy. One lumbar puncture (LP), a spinal tap done without a hitch, took forty-five minutes to an hour to complete. And she asked me to do three. The phlebotomist drew blood for routine studies, but the more invasive tests had to be done by the MDs.

When I was a medical student, I shied away from procedures that involved sticking people with needles. The anatomy under the cover of skin was still hazy for me. Now, I couldn't hide.

"Doctor, it's so hard to get the other house physicians to do LPs."

Because we didn't want to die! Here, nobody wanted to do any procedures if they could avoid it. We'd studied for so long, and then this HIV plague came along. Just one needle stick, and then it's adios to the many years of hard work, dreams of a successful career *and* a healthy life. Getting stuck, being exposed to infected blood and body fluids, was not just an occupational hazard but a death sentence for all health-care workers. There was no cure.

The medical community was waging a war against HIV. PA Hilde was the lieutenant who dispatched orders. I was the grunt, albeit a skilled one, who carried out the orders.

See one. Do one. Teach one.

This was the battle cry passed on from attending physician to the senior resident, to the intern, and finally, to the lowly medical student. Competence and independence were required to quickly move up the ranks. At this point, altruism and compassion were just marketing tools.

Students, interns, and residents vied to gain experience during training. We had to believe the slogan. We learned to diagnose quickly and choose the best strategy to ensure survival. With each skill under our belts, we eagerly pursued the next one. Being familiar with all contingencies saved lives.

Arrogance in believing that one can handle any medical situation is a necessary personality trait that, if not already inborn, is developed during this incubation period. Without the confidence to act, a physician is useless in an emergency situation. That's when doctors start thinking of themselves as God, or at least godlike. A medical doctor has to transform from grunt to God in less than five seconds. In medical school, I grew a small testicle.

At work, I ran around like a racehorse with blinders, targeting my finish line, my to-do list, organized at the beginning of every shift. I sprinted to complete my scheduled duties since unpredictable obligations always came up as the day progressed. New patients were admitted. Families wanted information. Patients died.

At the start of my twenty-four-hour shift at 7 a.m. on this same Thursday, I received a list of tasks to be completed from the outgoing house physician, Dr. Soonan. He then told me some shocking news about Bill, one of our colleagues.

Bill Arnaught was a Vietnam vet, six foot five, a full foot and four inches taller than me, and twenty years older. He had a prominent hawklike nose overlooking his straggly mustache. His shoulder-length salt-and-pepper locks made up for his receding hairline. With his less than lily-white lab coat, he was the epitome of an overworked but competent doc. His barrel-like frame was both commanding and congenial. He exuded the message: *You can trust me. I know what I'm doing.*

Arnaught was happy-go-lucky and irreverent with a personality as big as his booming voice. He talked a good game and won many an argument by volume alone. He had survived the rigors of war and then went on to become a doctor. Impressive. I never talked to him about his war experience, but darkness was never apparent in his demeanor. I envied his confidence. Life-and-death situations didn't faze him.

He had some eccentricities. His routine medical orders were word-for-word, straight out of a handbook, *The Washington Manual of Medical Therapeutics.* Looking at reference texts was common, but copying instructions verbatim raised my curiosity. With as much experience as he touted, why did he need to do that? Despite a carefree attitude, he did his best for patients.

He'd once called the Centers for Disease Control and Prevention to get advice on how to treat a certain set of HIV symptoms. This mecca of health information would surely be at the forefront of how to optimize medical care during this HIV pandemic. Surprisingly, the doctor he spoke with told him, "You're in the midst of this crisis. *You* tell *us* what works."

Another time, Bill had a female patient with vaginal bleeding. The gynecology consult would not transfer her to the gynecology ward, insisting the patient be cared for in the general medical unit—on Bill's watch. After much loud back and forth, Bill asked the East Indian doctor on rotation that night, "Do you know why you have that red mark on your forehead?" He was referring to the red bindi.

"No," she answered, perplexed.

"It's a target!" Bill barked as he stormed away.

Dumbfounded, she watched him disappear around the corner. Because Arnaught had been in a real war, no one thought about reprimanding him. He was broken, but no one was going to fix him. The Vietnam vet status provided him a lot of freedom; he was a good doc who wanted to save lives. Bill represented a distortion of the ideal physician, who had well-kept features, always wearing a crisp, white lab coat, and who spoke with a polite, soothing manner. He was caricature, but I considered him a medical deity. He reached a status I strived for.

All these thoughts passed through my mind as I heard the shocking news that Dr. Soonan delivered to me: Dr. Arnaught might not have been a real doctor.

No one explained what happened. Maybe he wasn't licensed. Or maybe he never went to medical school. I wondered if he was even a vet. Bill's disappearance didn't answer questions about who he really was, but it confirmed that he didn't have medical credentials to be treating patients. It seemed to me that the administrators just swept the sordid mess under the table, not wanting any headlines to reveal that their patients, who were mostly indigent, received suboptimal care.

So much always happened in one day, but that Thursday was the day I started doubting my choice to become a doctor. I could deal with the stress of being in the middle of an HIV plague. Doctors dealt with overcoming disease. I learned to treat patients. I got used to working twenty-four-hour shifts. It was my image of doctors that was being challenged. Seasoned doctors were supposed to help the sick and not hesitate to do their jobs. A person who I felt to be a good doctor was no longer allowed to work in the hospital. Bill Arnaught impersonated a doctor, and he did it with more confidence than I did. Did I belong here?

During astrology class, Iris described each planet as having personality characteristics with which we could identify. The planet Saturn was a stern teacher who presented obstacles to bring out Saturnian traits of being reliable, practical, persistent, and hardworking. I persevered during medical training. I didn't quit because it was practical to have a job. I learned to be a responsible and compassionate doctor despite my self-doubt that I wasn't good enough. I just strived to be better at my profession.

She would tell us, "Look at where the planets are in your chart." She held our attention and made the class interactions more meaningful because the subject was us. As we learned the meaning of each of the planets, we gained insight into our lives.

While learning more about astrology, it was hard not to be introspective and see how the rules applied to our lives. I started examining my past actions and seeing how they fit through the lens of the horoscopic chart.

Chapter 2:

The Big Apple

*H*onk. *Ho-o-o-onk!*
A cabbie snarled, "*Hey*, ya know what a green light means?" His car screeched past me to catch a fare on the northwest corner of Twenty-Ninth Street and Lexington Avenue.

The momentary shock woke me from my post-call haze. Since being done with my shift, I'd been on autopilot thinking about the past twenty-four hours—people dying, lumbar punctures, and Dr. Arnaught being a fake. I didn't even remember how I got from the hospital onto the train. All of a sudden, my stop, Lexington. As the station came into view, I reflected on how unfair it was that this fake doctor could do the work competently that I struggled with.

Once I looked up, it occurred to me—I almost got hit! I had to pay more attention and not just follow the crowd herding across Lexington, racing to get ahead of the "don't walk" sign.

How did I get here? A question I kept asking myself. While waiting for the walk signal to light up, the beating of my heart evoked memories from the past two years that gave me a familiar jolt. In a flash, the shame of having to take the orthopedic surgical rotation again and almost quitting medical school with only six months to go washed over me. I had never failed any course of study. My ego railed against this humiliation.

With only six months to go before graduation, I planned on quitting medical school. I went to my guidance counselor to let her know. During our discussion, she asked me about alternate plans for the future. The old fantasy of going to New York City to become a ballerina came out of my mouth. I blushed; there was minimal evidence of physical grace that would support any notion that I could make a living in the world of dance.

I chuckled to myself recalling how I turned to prayer for solace before my appointment with my guidance counselor, a habit learned from parochial school education. At the time, I likened my situation to the agony of Jesus Christ in the Garden of Gethsemane and continuously chanted, "God, if it's possible, let this cup pass from me." The second part of the prayer was always left out: "Let your will, not mine, be done."

"One year, that's all you need to do, then you can do anything you want." That's what my med school guidance counselor advised to me after hearing about my plans to quit school. "I've already mailed recommendations to the residency programs you listed. All you have to do is file your application." She ignored my rambling about being a ballerina. She explained that being a US graduate allowed me to get a license to practice medicine after one year of postgraduate training. Foreign-trained physicians had to retrain in a US-accredited program prior to being eligible for licensure. "All you have to do is finish one year. Then you can do what you want because you can support yourself," she repeated.

Honk. Ho-o-o-onk! These taxicabs were like geese being kept from flying through traffic. People rushed past me on the crosswalk. This was not the place to be lost in thought. Everybody had somewhere to go and didn't want to be late; not a second of the walk sign was to be wasted.

After reaching the other side of the street, I thought of a medical school joke that rang true: What do you call the person who graduated last in their class from medical school? The answer: a doctor. I did exactly as my counselor advised. I persevered for a half a year more, graduated later in 1989, and got accepted in an internship position in New York City.

It was 1989 and I didn't know what I was getting into. When I arrived in New York City, AIDS was on the rise and my Midwestern medical school, Indiana University (IU), had provided little experience in dealing with the virus. By the time I graduated, IU had treated only one known HIV case, a woman who had just delivered a baby. I had no contact with her. She was kept in isolation on the gynecology ward, and only the attending physicians treated her. From then on, the use of gloves became mandatory even for minor procedures like drawing blood for tests. Before, I never thought twice about getting blood on my hands.

Large cities were especially prone to the rapid spread of infection due to the high concentration of people. AIDS was incorrectly nicknamed "gay cancer"; the disease was indiscriminate. It was prevalent in any population that practiced injection drug use and sexual promiscuity.

Medical programs in the big cities were high-risk settings and had difficulty recruiting United States–trained graduates. We had a choice, and most of us opted to practice in areas with less exposure to the virus. Cuts, infections, and accidentally getting stuck with needles were once occupational hazards for the health-care community; now they were potential death sentences.

Out of close to two hundred classmates, two of us traveled to New York City from Indianapolis, Indiana, to continue training. My criteria for choosing a big city were simple. I didn't want to compete for a postgraduate intern position, and, when not working, I wanted to enjoy myself.

The internal medicine program in Brooklyn readily accepted me. In 1989, New York State had adopted the Bell Commission's recommendations that physicians-in-training could not work more than twenty-four consecutive hours, or more than eighty hours per week. The commission's conclusions were made following the investigation into the death of Libby Zion, who was under the care of residents and interns believed to be overworked. This landmark case recommended guidelines that initiated regulatory reform in physician training. How lucky was I to fall under this jurisdiction?

However, in the job interview at the Brooklyn Medical Center, the administrators made sure that the residents knew their institution didn't adhere tightly to the Bell Commission's recommendations. The guidelines weren't law. Trainees needed to follow their patients through the acute clinical course. *Continuity of care* was the catchphrase bandied about to justify unpaid overtime. To enrich the clinical experience, working hours would not be arbitrarily limited. Interns and residents would go home when done with their work. I agreed to that provision and also consented to night duty every third working day.

Chapter 3:

Informed Ignorance

During my internship year at Brooklyn Medical Center, I was getting used to being in a high state of anxiety, but I paced myself. I expected to race to finish the routine work of stabilizing patients. I expected to be interrupted by urgent matters. And I expected to be shamed at what I didn't know.

During medical rounds, the daily walking session with the attending physician overseeing the work of the residents and interns, we discussed how each patient was progressing, or not. It was a teaching session for the most part, and no one was exempt from being pimped—singled out and asked detailed questions about patient status. We were expected to do routine patient care and also read about all aspects of the medical conditions that necessitated admission, including past medical history, complications, and the side effects of the drugs being prescribed.

I was an excellent student before medical school because I could memorize easily. But the sheer volume of clinical information that needed to be incorporated and regurgitated at a moment's notice overwhelmed me. I couldn't memorize all the textbooks.

During one cardiology session, Stephan, another intern, stepped in when a question was thrown in my direction about a medication. He answered what was asked and then discussed the pros and cons of agents for hypertensive emergencies, anti-arrhythmic medications, and even compared the intricacies of centrally and peripherally acting drugs.

The cardiology attending's comment before explaining why he chose the specific treatment was a glib, "So, you've been reading."

After the meeting, I thanked Stephan. "You gave us a mini-lecture. You're a god!"

"Well, I'm sick and tired of them pimpin' us. They just have more experience than we do." That statement stuck with me, giving me a new perspective. My shortcomings were part of a phase that would pass with time and experience.

The HIV and AIDS epidemic highlighted the infectious disease (ID) specialty in the training program. We were all eager to learn how to control the virus. The ID attending, the medical doctor supervising the residents-in-training, was popular because he shared information and treated interns and residents as colleagues, not trainees. He updated us on the treatment protocols that were being established to control the disease, describing a flowchart on how to approach a set of symptoms that helped us develop our diagnostic skills.

While discussing a complicated case, the ID attending asked for my opinion about what organism might be causing the patient's fever. In any immunocompromised HIV patient, there was a host of possibilities. I couldn't organize my thoughts as coherently and quickly as Stephan could. To save myself from embarrassment by rambling and stuttering, I just said, "I honestly don't know."

The ID attending then confided, "I don't know either." His admission was refreshing. He showed no shame. In turn, I wasn't humiliated since he didn't see my answer as a weakness. It was just a fact. Not every question had an immediate answer.

But my relief was blunted because I knew it wasn't so. I could joke with this doctor as a colleague: "You don't know what the organism is, but you know what it's not. I don't know because I dunno. Yours is an informed ignorance. I'm just ignorant."

"You'll get there."

My perspective shifted. My confidence as a doctor was growing.

In 1997, I transferred this way of thinking to my astrology class too: informed ignorance. I liked that term. To me, it meant "still learning but not yet there." That's how I described myself now, studying this new subject considered chicanery, at best entertainment. Astrology interested me more than the other fortune-telling arts. It seemed to be the most scientifically based.

There was no prerequisite training required for Iris's classes, and they didn't follow a specific schedule or progression of topics. The lessons were based on what constellation the Moon was located on that day or what constellations dominated the "planetary weather," the activity above the clouds.

Instead of describing the day as "sunny and seventy-three degrees, with a warm breeze bringing in moisture from the southeast, coming in from the Atlantic," she would start a session with, "It's July. Today, the Sun is in Cancer. The Moon, Mercury, Venus, and Mars are also in this sign. The universe has chosen the topic of discussion. Today we'll talk about the sign of Cancer, what it means, and how it affects your life."

Iris glossed over the basics and spent a lot of time on interpretation, which was the more valuable information in my opinion. I could piece together the fundamental material on my own through basic science texts. Astrology was based on astronomy. Astronomy was easy to access.

I started to learn the anatomy of astrology to clarify my notes from Iris's classes. Instead of studying the structure of the human body, I was learning the framework of the topic: the planets, their function and meaning. Basic astronomy included facts about the planetary cycles in our solar system. The path of the planets around the Sun is called an ecliptic. It can be visualized as a leather belt encrusted with planetary gems spinning around the Sun and held in place by its gravitational pull.

Three-dimensionally, a merry-go-round came to mind, with several rows of horses rotating about a fixed center. There were different-sized creatures. Some of them were adorned with bright headpieces, but all of them were colorful with distinct characteristics. I always raced to ride the creature that moved up and down its pole. The planets were like that. They wobbled, seeming to move independently of one another, but were held together at the center by the Sun to a predictable route.

Then, there was the mythology to assimilate—the stories associated with these objects in the sky. The planets (Mercury, Venus, Earth, Mars, Jupiter, Saturn, Uranus, Neptune, and Pluto) and luminaries (Sun and Moon) were rulers identified with Greek and Roman gods and goddesses. The twelve constellations (Aries, Taurus, Gemini, Cancer, Leo, Virgo, Libra, Scorpio, Sagittarius, Capricorn, Aquarius, and Pisces) were their indentured serfs, identified with the mission of their ruler. Each planet and its associated group of stars represented traditions, specific beliefs, and archetypal personality traits.

The zodiac is the circular belt divided into twelve sections, or houses. Astrology compartmentalizes the constellations, assigning each of them to one of the twelve houses based on birth data. The occupants, or planets, live in the different houses reflecting the sign in which they were located at the time of a person's birth.

Many terms denote the same concept: zodiacal chart, astrological chart, and horoscope. *Constellation* describes the pattern of stars in the sky, while *sign* is the term used when referring to a section of the astrological chart (diagram) to which the constellation is attached.

I was used to describing things by several names. The stomach, for instance, can be referred to as an abdomen, belly, gut, tummy, paunch, and even breadbasket. A doctor could be called a physician, a medical practitioner, a specialist, a surgeon, and sometimes a quack. Learning specific language and context is necessary in order to become fluent in analysis and discussion of any topic being studied. It would've helped me with Jana, the first astrologer I consulted, if I had been familiar with the nomenclature.

This independent study was a lot of work for a hobby, but it was less stressful than medical training. Nobody died if I made a mistake.

The prediction aspect of astrology was appearing to be less and less like magic. To be a good practitioner in any field, one has to gain proficiency, learning the basic tenets and then being able to filter layers of information to focus in on a reasonable conclusion, prophecy, or diagnosis—terms that can describe the same concept.

I understood that planets could emit radiation with possible far-reaching effects that were difficult to quantify. I understood that the ancients associated the planets, the Sun, and the Moon with human characteristics based on observation. Was there a quantifiable, scientific basis for the connection?

In class, Iris had said, "Astrology isn't just reading a static diagram. The planets don't stay in the same place they were located when you were born. They rotate and their energies interact with each other. It affects us on Earth. If you don't believe me, think about the Sun. You can see the light and feel the warmth. And if you stay out too long, you get sunburned. The Moon affects water. Its gravity will cause high tides. You don't think it affects the baby in the womb?"

I understood the theory, and I was willing to accept the assumptions to see if astrology worked. The houses represent different aspects of a person's life. The astrological chart proposes to describe me at the time of birth. This was static information, like findings on an X-ray. If the heart is enlarged or if there is a pneumonia, it's indisputable. It's hard evidence. With tangible medical intervention, the person's clinical condition will change as well as the radiographic results.

What I wanted to understand was how the static information from the time, date, and location of my birth could be used to extrapolate and anticipate future events under the guidance of planetary movement. What was the planet's intervention? What energies were at work?

In my arrogance, with an MD after my name, I thought that I wouldn't need to be at my sharpest when pursuing this diversion. It was clear that my interest was becoming more than just a hobby. Sifting through facts mixed with mythology required mental dexterity, combining curiosity with imagination.

The poet William Blake said, "What is now proved was once only imagined." Not informed but enlightened ignorance is what I was now seeking. I hoped to get there.

Chapter 4:

A Crossroads

To keep the stress of work out of my personal life, I developed a ritual: when I got home, the first thing I did was take a shower. It washed away any residue from the hospital, as well as symbolically cleansed my spirit. I made it through another day. No one coughed in my face, and I didn't get stuck with any needles.

My friend Daniel wasn't so lucky. He was one year behind me in medical school and came to New York City wanting to experience the urban lifestyle, like I did. I met him during college. He described himself as a farm boy. Despite his description of country bumpkin parents, they provided well for him and his older sister. I never liked that he called his parents "hicks."

He was a charmer, good-looking, and funny. In the last year and a half of college, he discovered that he was gay, and the farm boy transformed himself into the ideal male model. His look was complete with clothes straight out of a Ralph Lauren collection.

He interviewed for a surgical residency with St. Vincent's Hospital in Manhattan. The medical school was in the middle of the city in the thick of the HIV epidemic. He raved about how well he was treated. As a US graduate, he was assured a spot. He wasn't yet a bona fide surgeon but already was a "golden boy," a sarcastic term we used to describe our arrogant classmates who looked and acted the part of a doctor even before graduation. Once he got to New York, however, he got caught up in the whirlwind of the city, partying whenever he had free time. We had long since stopped going out together. I just did not have the gusto he had for dressing to the nines and going out at all hours of the night.

One afternoon, he surprised me when he called to visit. He sat down in the living room of my five-hundred-square-foot apartment and announced, "I'm quitting the residency program."

Dumbstruck, I thought about all the time we'd spent studying. I searched his eyes waiting for him to say, "I'm kidding." It had been his life's dream to have the prestige, position, and title of surgeon. There was only one thing that would make him quit. "When did you test positive?" I asked.

Quitting patient care was the right thing to do. He didn't have to tell me that he didn't contract the virus while working. We didn't talk about where he was going to live or what he would tell his parents. All he told me was, "I have things planned. I've already collected morphine vials. If the symptoms get too bad, I'll use them."

We ended the visit with me saying, "Take care of yourself." He never contacted me again. Perhaps I was a reminder of a future that was never going to be.

It was hard to get away from HIV. Iris described that, in any relationship with friends, family, or lovers, when your rising signs are compatible you grow together, but then there are signs that grow together only to a point.

Both Daniel and I had had the same goal. We took a straight path. With the support of our parents, we were able to go from college to medical school. As students, we lived in the "two-four room," our nickname for the twenty-four-hour study area of the main library on campus. We commiserated when we thought we failed exams and were triumphant when we got our acceptance letters. But in New York City, our paths diverged.

Learning to prepare with what was under my control and to anticipate situations was a habit carried over from clinical work. I familiarized myself with my surroundings. In the borough of Manhattan, the major streets are all parallel or perpendicular. All avenues run north (uptown) to south (downtown). Streets always run east to west (crosstown). With the exception of large cross streets that run in both directions, even-numbered streets run toward the east and odd-numbered streets run toward the west. Fifth Avenue separates the east and west sides, and Broadway cuts through the city on a diagonal. Being acquainted with boundaries helped me navigate life and New York City. My strong Saturn always made me aware of limitations. Being detail-oriented reflected characteristics of having the constellation of Virgo ascending on the eastern horizon at the time of my birth.

My path was not always smooth. There were unseen obstacles in my city wanderings, doubt at my ability to become a good doctor, fear that other people would think the same, and fear of getting infected with HIV. Sometimes, I couldn't avoid potholes, which got me to ponder whether I could find a road that was not so rough, that would allow me to cruise along and just enjoy the ride unencumbered. Although my route was not as direct as I planned, I realized all I needed was a few rest stops to collect myself before continuing on.

Daniel's vision got distorted by the New York City lights. My friend got lost in the nightlife. As strong as his mind was, he forgot his body was not invincible. He hit a roadblock and was forced to make an exit, not a detour. I don't know what Daniel's rising sign was; all I know is that our paths branched at some point, never to intersect again.

I finished my internship in the summer of 1990 and opted to forgo the second and third years of the internal medicine program. The work schedule didn't bother me. I had second thoughts about my chosen specialty. I liked to ponder options. Thinking on my feet wasn't second nature; working in a constant state of chaos and needing to make decisions swiftly made me anxious. Indecision could cost lives.

At the end of my intern year, the assistant director of the resident training program called me to his office and asked a question I didn't know how to answer: "What are you going to do after this intern year?"

"I'm not sure, but if I stay another year then I'd have to stay the third. It'd be a waste not to finish the last year." I had the presence of mind this time not to mention pursuing a dance career.

He surprised me, insisting, "Why don't you just plan on staying this second year, and if you find another opportunity, change your mind."

"Thank you, but I don't want to sign a contract if I'm not going to keep it." To me, this option reminded me of staying in a romantic relationship just for the sake of having a relationship. I had no plans, but my heart wasn't in it. It was scary, but the door to this obligation had to be closed, even though I had no backup plan as a means to make a living.

I had a friend, Breina, another first-year intern who was confident of her medical skills. As a US graduate, she'd already gotten her medical license and secured a job in Brooklyn. She told me she didn't need to finish a three-year program and looked to take on a second position. "There are job openings in the Bronx," she told me. I pursued the opportunity, and that's how I became employed at the Bronx County Hospital as a house physician.

House physicians were the independent workforce, not involved in the training programs, created to address the concerns of the Bell Commission. We backed up the doctors-in-training, taking over their duties so that the medical institutions would be compliant with the commission guidelines. The position allowed me to make a living, working twenty-four-hour shifts a couple times a week, while deciding what to do with the rest of my life.

Saturn was placed in the fifth house of my chart, which represented education. Jupiter conferred luck and lived in my sixth house of service and health. Having met Saturn's challenge, I finished my internship year and was able to get a license allowing me to work as a physician. Lucky Jupiter and Breina helped me find the job opportunity. Mars, home in the sign of Aries located in my eighth house, was activating my transformation. I started gaining more confidence as a physician.

Chapter 5:

Walking Meditation

It had been about a month since I learned about the scandal around Dr. Arnaught. As a house physician, once my shift was over, the responsibility of taking care of patients was transferred to the incoming team. It was an efficient system since the primary treating physicians were not overworked. The disadvantage is that the patients didn't always have a familiar face to interact with. For me, I could have free time without worrying about continuity of care.

"You look like a well-dressed homeless person," my roommate joked on my way out the door to tour the city. "Or Garfield the cat," she said, referring to my favorite uniform when not working—a poofy pumpkin-colored hoodie. Winter of 1991 hadn't quite transitioned into spring yet, so my coat was appropriate. It was a sunny Sunday morning in March, and in the streets of New York City nobody would be giving me a second look.

"Where are you going?" she asked.

"To Eighth Street. I just gotta walk. I'll be back later."

"You wanna go to the Tibetan restaurant for dinner?" she asked.

"I'm meeting Sunil later and we'll probably get something to eat. I don't know when I'll be back."

"Okay, see ya!" she answered as I closed the door.

Our building was located on the southwest corner of Twenty-Ninth Street and Third Avenue. The United Nations Plaza was located on First Avenue and Forty-Fifth Street, northeast of our apartment. NYU Medical Center was two blocks due east. My commute to work would've been so convenient if I had applied and been accepted to NYU. Oh well.

I was headed south toward Eighth Street. At 10 a.m., the neighborhoods were ready for business. The Japanese and Indian restaurants awaited the lunch crowd. Korean grocery stores partially occupied sidewalks with stands filled with flowers and fresh fruit. Their doorways framed miniature buffet stations, set up with trays of chicken teriyaki, spicy beef, fried rice, mixed vegetables, and California rolls. Conveniently packaged selections were available for passersby who didn't want to take time to stop and sit for a meal, or for impulse eaters salivating at the sight of the colorful displays.

Walking was a meditation for me. Step by step, my feet propelled my body forward. People walked by and scenes flashed, accompanied by a cacophony of sounds from motor vehicles, all unobtrusive to me, like white noise. This steady stream of detail blurred and masked unimportant thoughts, allowing contemplation.

I had doubts about my life's direction. Being able to wear a crisp, white lab coat with my stethoscope necklace didn't stop the self-doubt. I wondered if being reliable and hardworking was good enough to be called a doctor? When had I decided to become a doctor?

In 1997, I decided to get a private astrological reading with Iris after taking a couple of her classes. She asked me questions to

verify the events of my early life with significant planetary configurations determined from my birth data. "What happened around
six or seven years old?" Iris asked.

"My family moved from the Philippines to the United States."

She explained, "Astrology is a map of your potential. Different
locations, different people will give different influences, good or
bad, depending on the circumstances presented. When you were
younger, your parents controlled the direction of your life. Your
mother and father influenced your destiny."

Manila, the Philippines, 1967

"It's Uncle Diko, Uncle Diko! He's here!" I yelled to anyone who
could hear me, pointing to the plane overhead. I was five years
old, and the fourth child, but I wanted everyone to know that I
was the first to see him.

"Hi, Uncle, hi!" I yelled to the blue sky while watching the
white tail of the aircraft grow longer. My three brothers and sister
would soon join me, running around in the concrete courtyard
between my mama's store and our house, greeting Uncle until the
trail dissolved.

Every time we saw a plane overhead, we would wave furiously
to greet the flying machine that represented my uncle. We yelled,
"There's Uncle, there's Uncle!" We never tired of the ritual.

My mother's youngest brother, Federico, nicknamed "Diko,"
was a faceless family member to me who had ventured to this vague
place, the States. I knew about America from television shows, and
Uncle lived there. I listened when my mom and dad talked about
how he had overcome obstacles and was now doing well as a *doktur*.

I didn't know what a *doktur* was, but if it meant I could fly in
a plane against the big blue sky like he did, I was going to be one.

I didn't know it, but my parents were already planning to
move to the United States. It would take them one more year

before my father's application to immigrate to the US would be approved. He did contract work for US Steel Corporation as a mechanical engineer. The company helped to secure his immigration documents by sponsoring him with a position in either the state of Indiana or the country of Malaysia.

Dad was the oldest of eight children. When his father died, he became a surrogate parent to his siblings. He wanted to attend medical school, but training to become an engineer took less time. He needed to work as soon as possible to support his family. My *lola*, my grandmother, relied on him to pay all the bills and keep his siblings in check.

Uncle Roming, who was the second-youngest sibling, once confessed to me, "I didn't like school. I was supposed to be in school, and your dad would check up on me. One time, he found me sleeping under a tree. After he woke me up, he gave me a belting that I never forgot." Uncle Roming's solution to both, school and my father's stern discipline, was to sign up with the US Navy. He lied about his age, saying he was eighteen years old instead of seventeen.

By the time my parents had me and my siblings, Dad had specific ideas of how to raise us. It was with a heavy hand. Discipline and education were stressed as the way to prepare us for life, but it wasn't going to be in the Philippines.

An incident occurred with the family business, a rice mill in a distant province, that my father also ran. He sent a cousin to carry a lot of money from the business located in the province of Batangas to a bank in Manila. When the cousin arrived in the city, the money was gone. He told my father that he'd been robbed. All the profit that came from the business was lost.

"*Bahala na!*" ("It's up to you!") Dad sighed harshly with a heavy heart and a backward wave of his hand. It was a gesture of disgust or surrender to some unseen force whenever he could not control the circumstances. He was tired of the burden of being a father to his parents' children. He had his own to care for. He took the theft as a sign that he had to get out of the Philippines to grow his own family.

So, in 1967, when I was five years old, my father moved to the United States to work at the US Steel plant in Gary, Indiana. He chose the United States over Malaysia because his youngest brother, who had immigrated several years before, had settled in Gary. Within two years, Dad saved up enough funds to be able to bring my mom and all the children to America. Our lives would continue in a new world.

But eight months after our arrival in the United States, I was involved in a car accident that almost killed me. Everything up until then seemed to be working out fine. With the advent of the new year of 1970, my parents bought a new home. Dad had a great job with US Steel. Mama worked as a registered nurse in a local hospital. The kids' routine was parochial school during the week and church on Sundays.

The accident occurred on a cool Sunday morning in July. We were going to church in Dad's new 1970 white Ford Falcon station wagon. I'd just turned eight during the past month, dressed in my favorite pink-and-white-checkered, seersucker dress, and patent leather shoes. As I walked down the steps toward the driveway, Dad had raised the hood of the car to check on whatever he'd been tinkering with the day before. At the bottom of the stairs, I turned around and reached up with my right hand to get the Sunday paper from the mailbox on the wall alongside the garage. Then, I blacked out.

The next thing I remember, I was lying on my mother's lap on the stairs inside the garage. She was crying and praying in Tagalog, "Have mercy on us, Lord. Alice, Alice, wake up. Come back to me. Come back to me." I saw my dad standing next to her, looking at me. He started crying, and then I saw my uncle talking to him. I wondered why he was here. There were a lot of neighbors in the garage. I was so tired. I went back to sleep.

When I woke up, I found myself lying on a table with bright

lights overhead, blinding me. I was surrounded by a lot of people telling me to relax. But I couldn't relax since they were cutting my favorite dress off me. Mom had had it made before we left the Philippines. I tried to get up and yelled as loudly as I could, "Don't ruin my dress! Mama! Mama!" I was fighting to prevent the man from cutting my dress. Two people took hold of my arms to restrain me. A plastic mask was placed over my face. I blacked out again.

I spent three months in the hospital where my mother worked. It took that long to heal the many internal injuries and right leg fracture that I sustained. Mom told me that while Dad was tinkering with the car, he accidentally placed the car in drive instead of neutral position while stepping on the accelerator pedal. The car careened down the inclined driveway and hit the left side of the garage wall with me in front of it.

Mom said that if I had died, they would have gone back to the Philippines.

A sparkle caught my attention as I continued on my walk. It flickered from the sunlight hitting a mirror in one of the funky boutiques. I was getting close to Eighth Street, also known as St. Mark's Place. The sidewalks got more crowded as lunchtime approached, but I maneuvered around individuals without breaking stride—like a true New Yorker! I passed more thrift stores, apartment buildings, condos, and about five Starbucks. Mm-mm, the smell of coffee was enticing, but marred by the exhaust fumes from the departure of flatulent city buses. I'd been here two years but still couldn't believe that I was living in New York.

Getting closer to my destination, I gravitated toward the upbeat rhythms of a steel drum with no sense of urgency. A street musician decked in colors of black, green, yellow, and red greeted onlookers with a ready smile and flirty eyes, cajoling them to make donations. Entrepreneurs sold their incense, trendy fashions, and homemade jewelry in makeshift kiosks. I fit right in with my loud, oversized sweatshirt. Day or night, this was my favorite place to be a passerby.

I looked around for the fortune-telling storefronts and the palm readers with their makeshift sidewalk offices that I had observed many times before, but never seriously considered consulting until now. Had my younger self been arrogant thinking that just because I was smart and had the ability to go to medical school, I could do the work? Was it too late to change direction? This was where I would look for answers. I would come back when I had more time.

Savory aromas from grilled food wafted into my nostrils, reminding me that I had to meet Sunil for lunch. We were med school classmates, and just before graduation, we found out we were accepted to postgraduate positions in New York City. He would be working at Long Island Jewish Medical Center as a psychiatry resident. He fit the New York scene immediately, driving his Porsche and wearing his clothes straight out of *Gentlemen's Quarterly* magazine. He also stood out since he had a long beard and wore a turban, signifying his Sikh religion. With his fancy car and charming personality, he gave off the aura of a genteel and intelligent socialite, which he cultivated. Perfect for his chosen profession. He laughed when I described him as "su-wa-vay" (suave) and "de-boner" (debonair).

Sunil frequented Manhattan. He was the Indian version of Speed Racer, the star of the 1960s cartoon series, in his fancy, fast car. He liked the city for all the entertainment it had to offer and also because the residents appreciated the status that came with his sleek, black ride.

From Eighth Street, I walked north and met him in a little hole-in-the-wall restaurant, easy to pass up with its narrow entrance, on Thirteenth Street between First and Second Avenues. The dank smell of stale alcohol from a previous incarnation as a bar couldn't be masked by the java that was constantly being brewed. The restaurant's dark wood interior led to a courtyard, flanked by walls from neighboring storefronts. Climbing ivy camouflaged the soot-stained buildings and the fire escape platforms on the upper-level apartments, giving the illusion of balconies. Subtle instrumental background music complemented the sunny afternoon. The noise of the city was kept at bay in this little haven.

The idea of the existence of some sort of manual for life came from Sunil. "Did you see the tarot card reader by the entrance?" I asked as he sat down.

Sunil sneered, "They're for suckers."

"Really? So, you have everything figured out, eh? What about your second wife?" I teased. He'd told me that he had a family astrologer in India who told him, "You will be married twice. One will be to an American and the second, your last wife, will be Indian."

Sunil scoffed at the idea. "Yeah, right. That'll never happen."

I argued, "But your family's been going to him for years. He must be accurate. How can you not believe it?"

He never spoke about astrology to me again after that. He was still single, but his life was already planned in his mind: finish training, make a living, marry—only once—to Sadhana, a beautiful, fashionable Indian woman he'd met in Queens, and then live a happily-ever-after life. His would be a traditional life, maintaining his family's religion and beliefs, but incorporating a modern lifestyle. Both worlds would coexist and not contradict.

At this time in my life, astrology was still entertainment and nothing more, found next to the cartoon section of the newspaper. But now, I had specific questions that couldn't be answered by conventional routes. I started looking more seriously at the signs advertising fortune-tellers, wondering if they could give me direction in life. I wanted to try them. I thought authentic practitioners were only found in India. I had limited income, so international travel wasn't in my future any time soon. I needed to concentrate on practicing my medical craft but still was curious about the subject.

"Hey, do you know any astrologers around here?" I asked, hoping Sunil would say yes.

"There are some astrologers in Queens, Jackson Heights, the Indian section, but I've only gone to the one in India. I'm hungry," Sunil grumbled. "Let's get food."

I was disappointed that he couldn't recommend someone. We were in New York City, with so many opportunities. Still, I was hesitant to explore the unknown by myself.

The divination arts—astrology, tarot, palm and psychic readings—fell under the veil of voodoo for me. *Woo woo medicine.* I didn't know what to expect. Would I be hoodwinked, fall under some spell, and tricked into giving the practitioners my last dollar? Were there secret doctrines that described the process of prediction and held keys to manipulating life's circumstances? I needed to know.

Chapter 6:

Ask, Seek, Knock

A couple evenings after my lunch with Sunil, I got definite leads to research the divination arts. Betsy settled into a chair in my apartment. She worked as an administrative assistant in the research department of Mount Sinai Medical Center and had become good friends with my roommate. She was fun and quirky, with her blond bob and signature pink lipstick. Since she'd lived in Manhattan for many years, I asked her if she had any experience with fortune-tellers.

"I have a regular astrologer who lives on the Upper East Side. She helped me through my divorce." Jackpot! Betsy was a believer.

"Is she a counselor too?" I asked.

"No, but she told me that I would feel better in about six months. And it took that long to work out our settlement. I'm a Pisces, what are you?"

"Gemini."

Betsy explained, "You're a Gemini since you're born in early June. If you're born in late June, then you'd be a Cancer. If you want, I'll give you the number of my astrologer."

Her referral started my contact with practitioners. Betsy wasn't clear about how she found Jana. All that mattered to me was that she had test-driven the mystery subject for several years and was no worse for the wear. Up to now, I'd just browsed through the occult sections of secondhand bookstores and libraries looking for information. I'd read about Evangeline Adams, an advisor to the banker and financier J. P. Morgan. The statement, "Millionaires don't use astrologers, billionaires do," had been attributed to Morgan. Evangeline Adams lived in New York City in the late 1800s and early 1900s. I would've loved to meet her, but Jana seemed like a good place to start.

Two weekends later, I was on my way to my appointment with Jana, walking west from my apartment to the Twenty-Eighth Street and Park Avenue subway station. I hopped onto the 6 train going uptown, got off at Grand Central Station on Forty-Second Street, and continued west, to Fifth Avenue. Heading uptown on Fifth Avenue allowed a scenic route, with Rockefeller Center on the left at Forty-Ninth Street, across from Saks Fifth Avenue. St. Patrick's Cathedral would be on the right at the next block.

It was chilly. My light jacket did little to block the cold breeze, especially when the tall buildings blocked the Sun. On the way back, I had to remember to stop and see if the ice-skating rink was still open at Rockefeller Center. It was only April. And I had to get my three wishes.

"Whenever you visit a new church, you get three wishes." It's funny how the things a mother tells a child become rituals. It doesn't matter whether or not they're true.

My leisurely stroll took me past Fifty-Eighth Street, providing views of Central Park greenery on the left until I reached the southeastern corner of Seventy-Ninth Street, my destination. I stood in awe, looking across the street at the magnificent columns flanking the entrance to the Metropolitan Museum of Art.

Despite the brisk weather, the steps leading to the Met bustled with activity. People read their newspapers, ate pretzels, smoked cigarettes, and socialized.

Time for my appointment. Business must be good, well enough to live on the posh Upper East Side across from the Met. In a doorman building. Hmm. Or maybe the home was from an inheritance? I turned around and entered the building, open to this new experience. No expectations.

Jana greeted me in her third-floor condo wearing a head-scarf and a flowy dress that I imagined a fortune-teller would be wearing. Then came the small talk for information to direct her reading. "What do you do? Why are you here?"

"I'm a doctor-in-training and interested in astrology. Betsy spoke highly of you," I lied. *You're the only astrologer I know, so I made the appointment.*

She then explained her process, telling me, "I've been reading astrological charts for over twenty years."

During the appointment, she first looked at both my palms, stating, "The hand gives clues about the person's life." Using a magnifying glass, she showed me the horizontal heart line that intersects with the longest, longitudinal life line on my right palm. The life line surrounds the puffy muscle at the base of the thumb, known as the Mount of Venus—the "thenar eminence," in medical lingo. It represents all things Venusian: romance, love, sensuality, and physical appearance.

Her face seemed sincere. She spoke English, but I couldn't understand the meaning of the astrological language she spoke. I laughed when she told me that having the constellation of Libra rising in the east at the time of my birth (my rising sign) made me attractive to men. I didn't know enough of the core teachings of astrology to have an opinion. It seemed like a general compliment that could apply to a lot of people to suck 'em in.

When she started talking about the medical aspects of my life, she was vague. Being familiar with my medical history, I felt she was fishing too much to get information to prove her point that my heavy menstrual flow was more serious than it was. She told me to get checked out. I wasn't having any problems, so I dismissed this information.

Jana used a lot of terms that didn't mean much to me, so I lost most of the details of what she said. After my appointment, I wondered if she gave the same information to different people. Could I spot the scam artist? I needed to do more research.

Betsy also gave me the contact information of a psychic, Guy, who lived in Little Italy.

She told me, "He never takes on new clients. When I called to make an appointment, I told him I saw him years ago and he believed me!" Laughing, she rationalized, "If he's really psychic, he should've known I was lying, right? Call him. Try to see him. He's good."

Why not? I don't remember what I said to Guy, but I secured an appointment the next weekend that I was off work. Riding the 6 train downtown and getting off at the Canal Street stop on Broadway took me to the border between two neighborhoods. North of Canal Street was Little Italy, and to the south, Chinatown. Canal Street in New York City had been an actual canal in the early 1800s, used to drain sewage to the Hudson River, but that didn't explain why Chinatowns in different cities all seem to smell like trash.

The familiar stench of pungent spices mixed with rotting garbage, made more putrid by traces of stale cigarette smoke and urine, evoked fond memories of my mother and father's shopping trips to the Chinatown in Chicago to get our monthly supply of Asian cooking ingredients. I was the only one of my siblings who would wake up early to go with them. Seeing the city skyline was worth the hour's drive from Gary, Indiana, and I always looked forward to lunch before heading home. Food and education. That's what my parents stressed. To think, you needed fuel.

Despite the offensive odors, I made a mental note to pass through Mott Street after my appointment and get some pig's ears, my mom's favorite. She cooked them in a pressure cooker, cut them into rectangular pieces, then pickled them in soy sauce and rice vinegar, adding diced raw onions for crunch. It was comfort food to me. My friends considered street food unsanitary. I never got sick.

I headed northeast from the subway stop toward the Basilica of St. Patrick's Old Cathedral. Guy hadn't given me an address. Nervous with anticipation, and because I was thirty minutes late, I was looking for "the only house across from the church near Prince and Mulberry" to call on a person who, supposedly, could tell me things about myself just by being in my presence. The cryptic directions along with other similar-looking buildings delayed my arrival. Finally, I knocked on the right door.

With a shock of curly black hair, darker than my own and which belied his age, Guy greeted me, saying, "Well, if you didn't show up, I would've just enjoyed my afternoon." I was relieved that he wasn't irritated and that I was the only client that afternoon. He wouldn't have to rush through my session to attend to another client.

He seated me in the dining room, filled with heavy hardwood furniture that looked like it had inhabited the room for many years. Diaphanous off-white curtains shaded the room with a soft glow. It wasn't hot outside, but it took me awhile to cool down from my hurried walk.

Guy disclosed that he had been a psychic to a movie star, predicting she would become royalty—which came to pass. Through his round dark-rimmed glasses, he observed, "You look very young, but I feel you have a very old soul." This stood out to me because the first book I bought when starting college, besides my textbooks, was Florida Scott-Maxwell's *The Measure of My Days*. Scott-Maxwell wrote this book in her eighties, and it befuddled me that as a nineteen-year-old I identified with her discussion about aging: regret that the physical body was slowing down while the mind became more passionate than ever about life.

Guy went on to say, "You're not going to meet any suitable romantic partners for a very long, long time."

Hmmm? Well, what does a "long" time mean? It was a vague prediction that didn't alarm me because, from my experience, when I worked toward something, I usually got it.

"Even from across the room, you can tell that they're not right for you." Also, vague. Hmmm.

I stayed quiet and observant, trying not to betray any clues with my body language. I looked to see how intensely he was looking at me, all the while wondering how he got the information and where it was coming from. It made me more curious about how fortune-telling disciplines worked.

How do these intuitives know what they know? I really didn't "see" what Jana, the first astrologer with whom I got a reading, and Guy were doing, but rather I experienced it. In making assessments about a person, palmistry had rules of interpretation related to markings of the hand, astrology used mythology associated with the planets, but psychic readings seemed to be the most subjective. I didn't see any visible use of aids, unless the intuitive was reading subtle body language. If thoughts come to them, how do they know what information applies to their client and what is just calculated guesswork?

As a doctor who diagnosed illness, I wanted to know the difference. More to the point, I wanted to know if this was a skill that could be learned. I needed more information to have an opinion, a perspective. I went to these different disciplines as a client interested in hearing what they had to say about my occupation. Was I supposed to be a doctor? I couldn't help being curious about their process. I ended up listening to their reading as well as trying to analyze and observe the practitioners for clues as to how they got their information. I wanted to ask practitioners how they got knowledge about clients, but the opportunity never came up. I didn't want to interrupt my reading and take them out of whatever state of mind they were in. I couldn't formulate any conclusions about their methods.

That's how it started. My New York experience represented an intersection. It's where I became a doctor but continued to look for something more. I took a detour but went in the same direction.

Chapter 7:

Handbook for Life

I n one class, Iris stressed, "The astrology that you read in the papers is just a small part of astrology."

My interest in prophecy started as a teenager when I discovered sun signs in the cartoon section of the newspaper, usually alongside a puzzle. I read it for fun, to see what the day held for me. It made me feel good that the outlook was always positive, but after the paper was laid down, no more thought was given to the daily prediction, and I went on with my usual routine.

Early civilization recognized the recurring patterns that the Sun and stars made in the sky. The Sun rose every twenty-four hours, but each day brought about different experiences. Every year brought about four familiar seasons, and each period varied annually in intensity and duration. Nature and the patterns of both the Sun and the Moon were integrated into daily life. Farmers learned to utilize indicators, like weather, to determine when to plant and when to harvest crops.

Before compasses, sailors relied on the positions of the spheres above the horizon to guide their vessels. The Sun rose in the east and set in the west. Polaris, the North Star, appeared almost directly above the North Pole after dusk. The constellation of the Southern Cross helped to locate the celestial south. Out of necessity, understanding the relationship of the objects in the sky with the environment on Earth helped early civilization survive. Today, use of celestial timing is still prevalent in the agricultural community. The periodicals *The Old Farmer's Almanac,* first published in 1792, and *The Farmers' Almanac,* published since 1818, provide annual calendars showing how the cycles of the Moon affect plant growth. There are also published articles on folklore, natural remedies, and weather. In addition, the almanacs talk about the best time to initiate certain activities for the best chance of success, which feels a lot like astrology to me.

Before my first astrology reading with Jana, the Sun and Moon were just constant fixtures of my environment. They were daily and seasonal clocks that sometimes evoked emotions. Sunrise was the constant harbinger of a new day. As a child, during June, July, and August, when the Sun was hotter, summertime meant school vacation, a respite marking the end of one school grade before passage into the next. I never spent much time outside after dark but often paused when the Moon was full, glowing against the night sky. The full Moon was romantic. I would feel a sense of buoyancy whenever I looked at sunsets, sunrises, and full Moons, and would automatically take in deep breaths to sustain that lightness. The other planets were part of the universe that didn't concern me because they were not easily visible.

During medical training, the Sun and the Moon were markers of day and night in the outside world. Inside the hospital walls, fluorescent lighting was perpetual, ignoring nature's schedule. I worked in a world that stressed technology to help patient survival using machines that allowed visualization of illness and analysis of the chemical composition of body fluids searching for abnormalities.

In her classes, Iris said that she wasn't a doctor and didn't give medical advice, but taught that medical astrology could be used as an adjunct to the field of medicine. She gave out a diagram showing which part of the body was influenced by which sign. She named the figure "The Astro-Man."

The Astro-Man

♈ ARIES

✦ Head
✦ Upper Jaw Palate
✦ Skull
✦ Eye & Vision

♊ GEMINI

✦ Respiratory system:
  Chest, Lungs, Trachea
✦ Neck, Esophagus
✦ Shoulders, Arms, Hands
✦ Nervous System

♌ LEO

✦ Spinal cord, Back
✦ Spinal column
✦ Heart, Vitality

♎ LIBRA

✦ Kidneys
✦ Groin, Loins
✦ Adrenal glands
✦ Lumbar region:
  Lower back
✦ Vaso-Motor system
  (Temperature balance)

♐ SAGITTARIUS

✦ Hips, Thighs, Buttocks
✦ Coccyx (tail-bone)
✦ Sciatic nerve
✦ Sacro-iliac joint
✦ Liver Hepatic system
✦ Arterial blood

♒ AQUARIUS

✦ Ankles, Shins
✦ Lower legs (calves)
✦ Circulatory system

♉ TAURUS

✦ Cerebellum (back brain)
✦ Middle ear
✦ Throat, Tonsils
✦ Larynx, Lower Jaw
✦ Salivary glands
✦ Thyroid gland

♋ CANCER

✦ Stomach, Breast
✦ Chest cavity, Ribs
✦ Pleura
✦ Mucous membranes

♍ VIRGO

✦ Sympathetic nervous system
✦ Small Intestine
✦ Pancreas
✦ Spleen
✦ Enzyme formation
✦ Antibody formation

♏ SCORPIO

✦ Reproductive System:
  Sex organs
✦ Excretory System:
  Bladder
  Rectum
  Lower intestine
  Colon
✦ Nose

♑ CAPICORN

✦ Skeletal system:
  Bones, Knees
✦ Teeth
✦ Skin
✦ Gall bladder

♓ PISCES

✦ Feet
✦ Endocrine system
✦ Lymphatic system
✦ Lymph and lymph gland

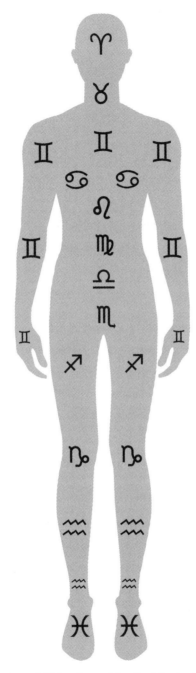

My version of "The Astro-Man" with glyphs identifying
the body area that each sign influences.

Aries, whose glyph is the horns of the ram, is the first sign of the zodiac. It heralds the spring season and represents the head and face. Taurus, which represents that natural second house of speech, is identified with the neck area, including the throat, vocal cords, and the thyroid gland. Gemini, symbolized by the twins, represents the arms, shoulders, hands, and the two lungs. Just as there is overlap when the seasons transition, there is extension of body boundaries. Gemini shares the chest area with Cancer, which rules the breast and stomach area. Although there are two breasts, which would be considered the realm of the twins, the symbol of breasts and the stomach are more commonly associated with the nurturing aspect of Cancer. Leo represents the spine in the upper and middle back, and the heart organ, symbolizing strength and emotion. Discriminating Virgo rules the abdominal contents of the small intestine, pancreas, and spleen. It is in the small intestine that nutrients are absorbed and separated from what is not necessary, which is sent along its way for elimination.

Scorpio, considered to be the most sexual sign of the zodiac, represents the reproductive system, including the sexual organs and the circulatory (blood) system. Libra, symbolized by the scales, rules the endocrine system, the lower back, buttocks, kidneys, skin, and spleen. From the endocrine system arises hormones that balance the body, including testosterone, estrogen, and insulin. The lower back contributes to the stability and support of the body. Capricorn represents the structure of the body, the skeletal system, including bones and teeth. Sagittarius influences the hips, thighs, buttocks, and liver. The calves, shins, and ankles link the entire body to the feet and are assigned to Aquarius. Pisces rules the feet and toes and therefore anchors the body to the Earth.

In the brain, different areas of the cortex, the outermost or superficial layer of the brain, control different parts of the body. My college neuroscience textbook illustrated a homunculus brain in which the various anatomical divisions of the body are represented on a map of the brain. The more complex functions of the body part correspond to a larger area covered in the brain tissue. The face includes the eyes, nose, lips, and tongue, which have more intricate motor and sensory function than the head or neck. The hand occupies more area of the cerebral cortex than the elbow, as it is capable of more purposeful movement.

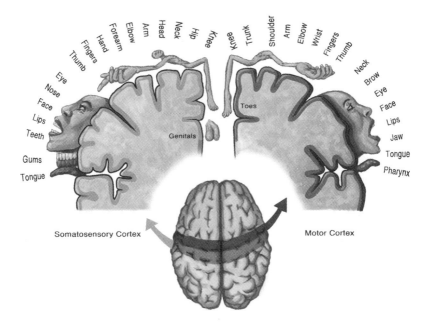

Homunculus Map demonstrating the regions
of the brain that control body functions.

The brain is the internal control of autonomic and voluntary body function. Autonomic nervous systems control body processes that don't require conscious effort, like digestion, blood pressure, or heartbeat.

When Iris presented the Astro-Man figure, I started seeing astrology as having an external influence on the function of the human body by way of the environment of the constellations.

Good health is multifactorial, influenced by the brain, the control center of the body, and environmental forces, including the distant celestial objects.

Iris mentioned that when a client requested a good day for surgery, she picked a date when the Moon was not in the sign representing the area to be operated on. "That's not the only thing I look at. There are other factors. A successful operation will also depend on your surgeon and the facilities that are available." Iris also analyzed the person's chart in the context of the whole chart of that day. In making medical decisions, she encouraged her clients to get their surgeons' birth data, if they were willing to disclose it, but also to research the physician's qualifications. In addition, Iris asked clients to find out what days their surgeons did surgery. "If the date I picked for a good result is on a weekend or a day when they don't do surgery, then I have to look at alternative dates." She clarified, "Use common sense. A lot of times, you can't get birth information. If you have an emergency and you have to have surgery, don't wait."

The topics of Iris's workshops always started with which constellation the Moon was located in on that day. Iris explained, "The Moon is the closest celestial object to the Earth and has the most influence on the human body. The different areas of the body are influenced by the Moon when transiting through different signs or constellations. It moves to a different sign every two and a half days, so the changes can be more easily perceptible than a planet such as Saturn that changes sign every two and a half years (meaning that Saturn stays in the same constellation for two and a half years). The planets affect environment, so they do have an effect on man in general. The water composition of the human body varies and can range from fifty to seventy-five percent. As the tides of the bodies of water on Earth are influenced by the Moon, so are our bodies."

I took in all the information Iris gave, but it wasn't feasible to test the surgery theory on myself as I wasn't planning on getting a lot of surgeries. It was easier to test astrology theory using the motion of the Moon, since its location changed every two or two and a half days.

I'd made a list of general trends Iris cited. Iris-isms, information that I could use on a daily basis to see if the rules worked. The collection would be the start of my handbook for life that I wished I'd had during medical training. I started integrating my activities around the signification of the Moon's location. I noticed I got a lot of work done when the Moon was in Virgo and Capricorn. When I would give lectures, I tried to schedule them on the day when the Moon was in Leo or Virgo. Leo was the showman, and I could project that in a lecture. The Virgo Moon would support my giving a detailed lecture. But a schedule couldn't always be under your control. As with any activity, you prepare and do the best you can.

The activity that was optimized corresponded with the personality assigned to the different signs. Iris had catchy descriptions of the Moon in the first three signs: "Aries starts the business, Taurus gets the financial backing, and Gemini will do the marketing." She also suggested optimal times to act. "Have a fashion show when the Moon is in Libra, but sell when the Moon is in Taurus. Have a party when the Moon is in Libra, not in Capricorn. A good day to take care of yourself is when the Moon is in your rising sign."

I read the daily forecasts in the newspapers less and less. As I delved deeper into the study of astrology, I found the newspaper astrology section to be pleasant and entertaining, not incorrect but generic and superficial. The myths of the gods' trials and tribulations were not just stories for entertainment. They reflected truths about the human condition, with the dramas of virtues and vices personified by the planets. These planetary myths were passed down from generation to generation by oral tradition before print was available. The astrology section relegated next to the cartoons belied its depth of history and wisdom.

Iris's workshops were scheduled intermittently and the topics presented in no specific sequence, so each class had new faces. Iris always gave a general introduction about astrology and what the planets signified, so participants were always oriented to the big picture. Many times, the participants had planets in the same sign where the Moon was located, and Iris would tell the class, "It's no coincidence."

After I greeted my classmates and revealed my occupation, they often expressed curiosity that a doctor would be open to such a mystical topic. They had the same reaction as I initially did, that the study of medicine and astrology were conflicting disciplines, until Iris mentioned that Hippocrates, named for the oath I took as a doctor and considered the father of medicine, was an astrologer.

Hippocrates insisted his students study astrology, saying, "He who does not understand astrology is not a doctor but a fool." He taught medical astrology, where the astrological signs, as well as the luminaries and planets, are associated with different parts of the body. Nature's influence on man was accepted and integrated into mainstream thinking.

With each class, the question "What's your sign?" took on more meaning for me. I started repeating Iris-isms, phrases that resonated with me. *Whatever you don't understand, you attract. Whatever you are drawn to, you need to learn.*

I thought about all the alternative practitioners I'd met before Iris and looked at my chart for clues. The ninth house signified father, gurus, higher knowledge, long-distance travel, and spirituality. The Sun represented authority, vitality, leadership, and strength. The Sun lived in the ninth house section of my horoscope with Mercury, the communicator, who represented intellect, education, curiosity, and adaptability. Together, they occupied the sign of Taurus, symbolized by the stubborn bull. If I had a desire to learn about a subject, I had persistence to look for answers from different teachers, no matter how unconventional.

That's how interpretation started, like painting a picture. The artist blankets the background with basic colors to give the observer perspective. Is the backdrop bright or dark, day or night? As layers of paint are brushed on, the scenery becomes more recognizable. Depending on the expertise of the artisan, he or she is able to apply subtle tints of color to bring out the details of a potential masterpiece.

In my study, the initial layers of astrological information fit. As a doctor, I achieved higher education with the support of my father, represented by the Sun. He was a traditional male in some ways; women cooked and cleaned and men made a living, but he was flexible in that he saw that I had potential to excel at the opportunities he wasn't able to pursue while caring for his siblings. Education was mandatory and my parents encouraged further study.

The Sun's vitality in the house of higher education supported my pursuits in that direction. My Mercury's position in the ninth house, in the sign of Taurus, reinforced that I had the intellect to investigate different types of knowledge. Taurus, symbolized by the stubborn bull, helped me to develop as a practical and reliable person, who plods along in pursuit of a goal. As a practical bull, before I explored alternative metaphysical disciplines, I made sure I had a day job that paid the bills.

Chapter 8:

Exploring Past and Future Lives

After my intern year, I worked twenty-four-hour shifts two to three days a week as a hospital physician. When not at the hospital, I spent time on my new interests. One of the people in my yoga class circulated a flyer for "Past life regression. Gain insights in this life by exploring previous lives." The notice advertised a weekend workshop in New Jersey. Why not?

My yoga friend didn't plan on coming but had been to workshops sponsored by the same woman and assured me the situation would be safe. The next weekend, I drove to New Jersey to participate.

The participants were encouraged to stay in the large home converted into a meeting place. Meals were included with the accommodations. This experience was going to be intense since the attendees would be together for the entire weekend.

The workshop was led by Roger Woolger, a psychotherapist and author of *Other Lives, Other Selves*. He believed in reincarnation; his therapy was based on the premise that recalling prior life experiences helped a person understand and even heal current life situations.

After Roger explained his work, we started. We were to find out about our possible past lives through a relaxation experience. We didn't introduce ourselves to the group so that there would be no preconceptions or ideas to influence our process. Our class of fifteen gathered round, reclining on the floor while being guided though a visualization exercise.

"Take deep slow breaths. Let your mind wander." After two or three minutes, Roger asked in his soothing British accent, in metered succession, "Where are you? Are you by yourself? What do you look like? What are you doing?"

After another ten minutes, he directed us to slowly sit up and write down what we "saw" and the emotions we experienced.

The man next to me described himself as a great baseball player. A woman across from me lived in Egypt as a slave during the time of Cleopatra. I envisioned an elderly woman that looked like my grandmother, with salt-and-pepper hair pulled back in a bun. She was gaunt with wrinkled features, in a well-worn sleeveless cotton dress surrounded by huge mounds of garbage. The person looked like my grandmother, but it felt like me. I felt the loneliness of this person. She had been all by herself most of her life. I felt the hunger pangs that gnawed in her stomach as she searched for food scraps in this wasteland. It was me!

After each participant reported their "memories," we voted to see which story would be developed by Roger. The group elected to explore my story.

I often took great effort to be the observer in any public demonstration, always staying in the background and hesitant to call attention to myself. However, in this case, my need for privacy disappeared. I was elated to gather more information about myself. During the drive from Manhattan to New Jersey, I'd set an intention to be open to whatever experience arose. I didn't know what the workshop would entail, but I kept repeating to myself, "I want to be picked. I have to find out if there is information that will help me get clarity about this life."

I took center stage because this was the only place where I would get knowledge of a past life. Without hesitation, I followed Roger's instruction and lay down on the carpet in the center of the group with Roger seated to the left of me.

As my head touched the pillow, I started crying. "They left me," I sobbed. "They left me. I'm eight or nine years old. I'd been playing in the woods and when I got back to our encampment, they were gone—my mother, father, brother, and sister. I looked at the area where there should be a campfire cooking food but saw only ashes. I kept turning all around looking at the clearing for any sign of where they were. No one. I was by myself. The next thing I see is myself running through the woods yelling, 'Mama, Daddy, Mama, Daddy!'"

"Where did they go?" Roger asked.

I didn't know from where I was getting my information, but there was no hesitation in my response. "We're wanderers living on land, eating plants. Sometimes my father would be lucky when hunting and we had meat. They left me. I don't know where they went."

All the while, I had parallel thoughts. I was born in the Philippines and then we moved to Indiana, but we always lived in houses. Dad never hunted. We'd never even gone camping. Once when I was a teenager, Mom and Dad drove me to summer camp, but I told them to take me back home when I saw how filthy the bathrooms were.

I was aware that I was on the floor and Roger was there, along with the other participants, listening to me as details poured out with no filter. "I don't know where they went. There was another family. I was supposed to marry someone from that family. But now they're all gone." The memories were so incorporated into my being that it felt as if the experiences happened in my current lifetime. It felt real.

While I relived this past life, my rational mind detached so I could be an observer to what unfolded with Roger's prodding questions, all the while aware that he was guiding me to a part of my brain that was not under my conscious control. I pushed aside the conflicting thoughts of this lifetime because I wanted to explore the movie that was unfolding behind my closed eyes—memories that Roger said were from a past life.

I didn't care what the other participants were thinking. My apprehension about being the center of attention had fallen away. I was more interested in the scenes and feelings that flowed as I continued to report what I saw. I wanted to stay in that space for as long as the motion picture would run.

"How are you surviving?"

"I have to take care of myself. All by myself. Sometimes I'd run through the forest and just scream for them to come back, but no one hears me. I haven't seen anyone else in so long."

"What are you doing now?" Roger asked.

"I'm still alone. Now I'm looking for food in these garbage mounds. I don't know how to hunt and there's been a drought, so there's not much vegetation."

It wasn't a dream. I was fully cognizant of being in the center of the group and the therapist inquiring about the scenes playing out in my mind. The thoughts and feelings of the mental movie occupied my senses, but my mind was able to separate and be a bystander. I don't know where the images and feelings came from, but the experiences felt like my life. A past life. Where else could these memories come from, with so much detail, so alien from my current life?

After Roger brought me out of my reverie, he said, "That's the fastest that someone has gone back to a memory."

I confessed, "On the drive here, I told myself to be open for something to happen."

"How does your past memory apply to your life?"

"Well, I'm very independent. I'm used to being alone. I have a supportive family, but my education seems to take me to places away from them. I often think that I will always be alone."

On the drive home, I questioned everything. Where the heck did all that come from? Was that really a past life? Is that really the reason why I make sure that I can take care of myself? Is that the reason why I'm always thinking about my next meal?

Before my year at Bronx County Hospital was over, I got accepted to a physical medicine and rehabilitation program specializing in nonsurgical treatment of musculoskeletal impairments. In 1994, I completed the training program as one of two chief residents at Albert Einstein College of Medicine in the Bronx.

True to the themes of my ninth house of higher education, I then relocated to Milwaukee to do further study of electrical potentials in muscles and nerves. In March of 1995, a couple of months before my electromyography fellowship ended, my friend Magdalena surprised me, calling me from Chicago to ask, "Do you want to see this psychic I know? Come visit."

She was also close to finishing her residency training and was looking for a job. I'd known her since medical school and never knew she had interest in mystical topics, but then, I never talked about my outside interest in this subject either. It was a happy coincidence. I'd always accommodated her when she'd suggested adventures. I'd just asked when and where to meet her.

Magda had already checked Sam out. She was vague about how she'd found him. "The last time I saw him, he was right on." About what and when, she didn't say. I guess we both felt that the less we talked about seeking answers from a psychic, the less we would need to rationalize it to each other. We made appointments and just went.

Despite being unsure of what to expect, I was always excited and curious to see how a new intuitive worked. I went to appointments with an open yet skeptical mind. It was interesting to hear what they would say about my life. After meeting with several practitioners, I could be objective about whatever they told me.

For a half-hour session, Sam charged fifty dollars. I traveled from Milwaukee to Chicago and met up with Magda. Then we drove to Cincinnati, Ohio, staying overnight at her parents' home before driving the next day to our appointments just outside Indianapolis, Indiana.

Sam lived an hour west of our alma mater, Indiana University School of Medicine. On the drive there, a wave of apprehension came over me as I started seeing gun racks in the back windows of passing trucks with bumper stickers supporting the National Rifle Association. A Confederate flag waved on a porch in a neighborhood we passed through. A couple of road signs, including the last stop sign, had dents. Good targets, I guessed. From BB guns, I assumed.

Although we'd gone to school in this area, I'd never ventured far from the city. We were two Asian women driving through the back roads of rural southern Indiana. Magda didn't seem to have the same concern. Her mind was occupied with following the directions to Sam's home.

As we continued, her calmness slowly washed over me. I noticed it was still cool this early spring afternoon. The heat hadn't yet caught up with the humidity, and I started enjoying the quiet ride.

Sam's home was on a peaceful tree-lined residential street, complete with a rocking chair on a faded wooden porch. There was no sign advertising any psychic business. We entered a neat living room through a squeaky screen door. The well-worn furniture included a couple of La-Z-Boy lounge chairs and small statues of Native Americans on the end tables. The open windows welcomed the afternoon breeze.

"Hello, which one o' you wanna go first?" Sam asked as a greeting. He was in his mid to late sixties, thin and balding, with a resonant voice that didn't match his slender frame. There were no specific physical characteristics to identify individuals with intuitive skills. I would hold my judgment on whether I could trust what he said during the reading.

I turned to Magda to make the decision. She nodded. "You, I'll wait."

Sam pointed my friend in the direction of one of the recliners and, in a thick southern twang, directed me toward the swinging door leading to a small kitchen. "C'mon. We goin' dis way."

I sized him up before entering the room. If anything bad were to happen, I could take him. When I saw a picture of Jesus Christ on a wall of the small room, I let out a quiet sigh of relief. Not everyone who had Christ's picture hanging so prominently was decent, but my bias was that if he was Christian, more than likely he'd be harmless and just give us our readings.

Curiosity replaced my apprehension. Looking around, I saw that the room was sparse, neat, and clean, with all the usual appliances, refrigerator, stove, and sink. Plain but functional. Sam directed me to a chair on the far side of a small round dining table, chrome rimmed with a white plastic finish on top.

As I sat opposite him, he pointed above my head and to the right. "That's ma spirit guide, Sweet Willow." My gaze followed his finger where a framed watercolor portrait of a young Native American girl hung. I stared at the familiar face with a bright, innocent smile. Except for the long braid lying over her right shoulder, it could've been me as a teenager.

Click. Click. My head snapped back to Sam. What he didn't explain was his metal noisemaker. He had his left hand on top of the table, but his right hand with the gadget was resting on his lap beneath the tabletop so I couldn't see what made the noise. The clicks were similar to the sounds of the colorful noisemaker toys I used to play with as a child just by pressing the gadget between my thumb and forefinger. Did it help him focus?

He started. "I'll be going through three levels of conscious, vibrational spirit. The third level is the spirit involvement wit' light only. From there, Sweet Willow'll be the one to open the veil and connect the cord, and I will be connected." *Click. Click.* "Your reading lasts a half hour. When she pulls the cord, I'm done. She'll give you the opportunity to ask questions 'fore she pulls it. And it may lead you ten years down the road. I don't know how they're gonna do it. And whoever does the reading, no matter you know them or what, they're only gonna touch you soul to soul. Okay. They're not touchin' the physical." *Click. Click.*

I tried to take in all that Sam told me while observing his process. Throughout my reading, he made eye contact with me and would return to the picture of Sweet Willow, watching for her signals as he asked for them.

I got used to the rhythmic clicks as part of the reading once Sam started to speak.

"Nothing happens till the appointed hour the soul's ready. Okay." *Click. Click.* "I'm not a hundred percent right, but I'm not here to prove nuthin' to anybody. I'm here to try to help ma fellow man sense his way through this opportunity." *Click. Click.*

"When I touch the vibration . . . You workin' now? Because I saw a change here in the work area. Okay. And you may have just changed a job, but then, there's a light. There's another change, touchin' with more money as you hit June. Okay. There's a light on the left. And when I touch the vibration. Give it again." *Click. Click.* "The job you're in now, you work directly with people, because I got service to the people, public? Okay?"

I nodded. What and where my future job would be was the information I sought.

I didn't speak or react unless necessary. Being skeptical had become a habit, so muting my responses became second nature so as not to give any clues from body language to inform his reading.

"And when I touch the vibration, this job you're on now. They have more than one location? Cuz I got more 'n one location here. Okay. And when I touch the vibration. Give it again. Have you ever worked for a city, state, or gov'ment? There was an eagle touched. Okay.

"And when I touch the vibration. You work for 'em now? Because there's a step coming, and I'll still go with May or June.

They're changin' somethin' that'll give you an opportunity. Okay."
Click. Click.

I couldn't follow the timeline of the events that Sam was talking about, but I didn't interrupt as he was on a roll.

"And when I touch the vibration. Give it again. I saw a trip touchin' in front of you. You take a trip to Chicago, up and back. It's a weekend thing. I'll leave it lay. And three of you go." *Click. Click.*

He was right. This weekend Magda and I had come from Chicago, and we'd drive up before the weekend was over.

Sam continued his reading, "You got any relatives or friends in California?"

"My parents and brothers live in California."

"'Cuz I had San Francisco and LA touchin'. Chicago touched in here. Do ya know anybody there? There's gonna take a trip there."

I pointed to the living room, saying, "My friend is from Chicago."

"You know anyone in Ohio? 'Cuz Ohio touched, and I had Dayton or Cincinnati. Okay. Columbus, also when I touched the vibration."

"Her parents live in Cincinnati."

"And when I touch the vibration. The east touched in here. Do you know anybody in Boston, New York, or New Jersey?"

"I used to live in New York City." Trying to direct the reading, I asked, "Where do you see me moving to?"

"Where will you be next year? Is that what you're sayin'? Well, when I touch the vibration, it feels like another move from where you're at. To another state. Okay. But I don't see you going back home. I don't see you going over water. Okay. But you may go to California. I'll leave it lay. 'Cuz California did touch. It hasn't let up. Okay. So, whatever I touch, when you make the move, this looks like you move outta state from where you're at and I'm not ruling out California, 'cuz it looks like you move there. Okay. And I got fall '95. Okay.

"You got any more questions? If not, Sweet Willow'll pull the cord and we're done."

I said, "No more questions. Thank you."

"Cord's pulled. We're done."

As I got up to let Magda have her turn, Sam also stood up, loosened the grip of his right hand, and laid a dull silver Zippo cigarette lighter flat on the table. So that's what made the clicking sound, the opening and closing of the lighter. I'm sensitive to the smell of smoke and didn't notice any lingering odor. Maybe because the windows were open.

I tried to listen to Magda's session but heard only indistinguishable conversation with the door closed. The chairs were comfortable, so I fell into a nap.

On the drive to her parents' house, we compared notes. Sam also mentioned California as a possibility for Magda's future.

Magda offered a possibility. "Did he confuse us? We're both doctors, same age and height, both Filipinas, raised and educated in the United States. Do you think we have similar destinies? Parallel lives? I guess we'll find out."

"That was fun!" I told her. "You know, he saw us traveling to and from Chicago! But he saw three of us."

Magda howled, "There are three of us. He saw Max." Max, Magda's German shepherd, would be traveling with us. He weighed eighty pounds, so he could count as another person.

I was stunned for a second, then I laughed with her. While reclining in the passenger side of the car, I mulled over the events of my appointment. For half an hour, I'd sat across from this simple old man wearing a Native American medallion around his neck, staring into space over my right shoulder, communicating with a spirit guide whose physical form was a watercolor portrait. I'd been more attentive because he spoke plainly with no technical jargon. He'd said so many things that could only be proved by time, but I believed him.

Magda had described Sam as a psychic. A psychic blends their energy field with that of the client's and is able to tap into a person's life and potential. Sam was more a medium who connected with the unseen world through Sweet Willow, his guide, his go-between. She was the medium for the spirit realm who allowed Sam to access client information at will. I didn't see him make any preparations. He didn't light a candle or chant to get into a certain frame of mind. He just sat down, explained what he was going to do, crossed a barrier imperceptible to me, and communicated with Sweet Willow.

Sam wasn't rude, but there was no chitchat either. I'm not sure he would have been able to explain how he interpreted the light he saw or the vibration he touched if I'd asked. His only explanation was, "I'm not here to prove nuthin' to anybody. I'm here to try to help ma fellow man sense his way through this opportunity."

Magda and I behaved like I used to, after perusing the daily horoscopes in the newspaper, happy to hear decent news about the future, but then going on with our daily lives. Sam told us about possibilities he foresaw, some linked with specific time frames, but he didn't tell us how to get there. The most important thing he gave us was hope that our efforts were not in vain.

Truthfully, we had marketable skills. There's no question that we were going to be employed. Sam's reading helped us approach the future with optimism. We still had to look for the opportunities, interview, and visit potential locations to live. Whatever would unfold was up to us.

Chapter 9:

A Stopover

So much had happened since last March when I met with Sam. *You move outta state, I got fall '95. Okay.* Here I am in Fort Myers, Florida. It was Magda who wound up in Northern California.

Sitting on the balcony of my second-floor, one-bedroom apartment, overlooking a busy side street, my thoughts strayed to dreams of living by the ocean. I would buy a home on the beach when I got more settled. Walking by the water's edge after a long day and feeling the breeze would make up for the hot, muggy commutes during my weekly duties at three offices, two hospitals, and one skilled nursing facility. It was just after two o'clock on a Sunday afternoon in late September in this early fall rainy season. My day of rest. Like clockwork, the afternoon showers started. Falling raindrops cut through the steamy air and felt like ants crawling on my skin. I didn't mind sitting in the rain. It was a pleasure to just sit.

The months from March up until now had been chaotic. By May, everyone who was graduating the residency and fellowship programs had lined up jobs before summer, except me.

I'd been too busy finishing my clinical projects, so that it wasn't until the end of May, a month before my apartment lease was up, that I contacted a headhunter. By mid-June, he offered me a contract to be a house physician in Portland, Maine. Then came the offer I wanted.

Vanessa had graduated two years before me in my specialty, physical medicine and rehabilitation, from the Medical College of Wisconsin in Milwaukee, where I spent my last year doing fellowship training. She contacted her previous professor, my mentor, asking if any of her graduates were interested in a Florida position. I accepted the job offer but wouldn't be able to start work for two or three months, the time it took to process a license application. For the interim, I had an idea.

The Portland hospital had reassessed its training program and was implementing the Bell Commission's guidelines to improve patient care by limiting residents' work hours. With my résumé listing past experience as a house physician in the densely populated New York City area along with completing a residency program, I could facilitate a smooth transition in the Portland hospital. It gave me the audacity to negotiate with the recruiter.

I agreed to work in Maine with the provision that when my Florida medical license arrived, I could leave without notice. Within a week, the hospital administrators procured a temporary medical license and rented a house and car for my use. The headhunter got his commission, and I would be spending the rest of the summer in New England with a Florida dream job in the works. Perfect.

The Florida practice was in desperate need of a rehab doctor. Vanessa had given birth in July with her first child, and her patients had no physician coverage. Trixie, the practice manager, called and asked me to fly to Tallahassee and hand-deliver my application to the Medical Board in hopes of facilitating early approval.

I ended up working in Portland for only one week before my Florida license arrived. I left the Maine hospital with no notice, no guilty feelings, and no repercussions.

By mid-August, I started working in Florida. My goal to live close to a beach was manifesting. This medical practice would flourish into a lifelong career, and my "forever home" would be by the water.

I expected to work by myself, covering inpatients and outpatients, as well as those admitted to skilled nursing facilities, until Vanessa returned from maternity leave. Vanessa resumed work in the fall, two months after I joined her business. Our schedules involved covering different duties on different days, and so it was rare to see each other when working. Yet I'd also expected to have some sort of welcome to meet my employers and get to know them once she came back from maternity leave. However, we never socialized. We never even had a personal conversation.

I only met Vanessa once, after she returned to work in November, three months after I started working for her. We crossed paths at the main office in the morning. She was seeing outpatients while I set out to do rounds on my hospital patients. She only asked if I was able to handle the work. I met her husband once, briefly in the office during the first three months.

All I knew of Vanessa was her work. On more than one occasion when covering for her patients, her reports would be missing. Her actions indicated to me that she wanted to be a full-time mother and not be occupied with a career.

I loved my profession and I expected to work long hours, but I couldn't tolerate the inconsiderate work environment. I could fend for myself in my private life, but with work, I expected to have some say. It only took six months for reality to settle in. My ideal job was only an illusion. Vanessa had an ambitious husband and an aggressive practice manager, with whom I also only had minimal contact. My role was to be an indentured apprentice to their future empire. I was an employee, with no say when my duties changed, such as what schedule was more convenient for me, considering my other duties.

In late November, as I walked into the office one morning, an office clerk told me, "Doctor, Trixie told me to tell you that you're supposed to go to this new office in Bonita Springs today."

I didn't know who my contact person was at this other office. I didn't know what the setup was or what equipment I needed to bring. Once I got to the new office, I had to find someone who knew why I was sent there. I found out I was to facilitate consults on the patients at that facility so that there would be no lag time in getting them to rehabilitation therapies. No other duties were taken off my schedule. I had to work everything out somehow. My employers just needed a faceless physician. I felt disrespected.

Trixie did not cultivate a healthy workplace environment. Publicly, she was all smiles, which hid her cutthroat personality. She focused on generating revenue with little thought to the welfare of her employees. She took pride in terminating personnel. Her assistant proudly showed me the axe pendant she received from Trixie after being delegated to fire a staff member.

My employers' ambition to create a Fort Myers medical dynasty relied on giving me as much work as possible. With Vanessa back to working full-time, they gave me another duty just as I was getting comfortable with my schedule. One February morning, I was called in to speak with Vanessa and Trixie. It was the second time I'd spoken with Vanessa and the first time they discussed any schedule change with me. Trixie did most of the talking. "We are going to start scheduling lunches for you with different doctors in the community to try to generate more business."

"I'm already working sixteen-plus hours a day, and I don't think I can do any more." I didn't mention that this was Vanessa's business and she should be promoting it.

"Well, just try it. Today, the lunch is at Olive Garden, one o'clock."

"That's the busiest part of my day," I pleaded.

Vanessa just sat there while Trixie said, "Just see how it goes," then stood up and walked away. There was no discussion. Vanessa followed without a word.

I waited for my lunch appointment for an hour before realizing I had been stood up. I had tried to be accommodating, but now I had to set boundaries. I called the office to set up a meeting for the next day with Trixie and Vanessa.

I told them both, "I don't have time to do public relations with doctors right now. I've got too much work to do to waste time doing lunches. It takes at least two hours out of my day. Sometimes I don't even take time to eat. Good work will generate referrals. I can't do the lunches."

"Well, okay," was all Trixie said. Again, no comment from Vanessa. I felt uneasy because there was no discussion. I wasn't satisfied with the outcome, but I felt pretty good standing up for myself. But I had a sense that Trixie gave up too quickly.

During times when I didn't know how to act or react to difficult situations, I just continued with the work that needed to get done. Throughout the rest of that workday, I thought of my early days in the Bronx, and similar emotions crept into my consciousness as I compared it with this job in Florida. The same anxiety and doubts welled up. Fort Myers, like New York City, seemed to be a perfect location to work. Being close to a beach was an added bonus. And just like New York City, the work situation wasn't what I wanted. But unlike New York, I had options.

In my chart, the tenth house assigned to Gemini represents career and how the world views me. The characteristics of Gemini include being a communicator, open-minded, and versatile, which I tried to be, but my employers were not interested in my point of view. Vanessa's bottom line was to create an empire with me being the workhorse. Nothing more.

The Moon in any chart is associated with mother, and Venus represents the feminine. These planets cohabitate my tenth house, accentuating my gentle nature. My quiet manner and small frame (I am five foot one and 115 pounds) may have given the impression that I can be easily manipulated. However, the planet Mars, representing the god of war, is strong in my chart because he is in the sign of Aries, the sign he owns. Together, they have the potential to unleash unbridled fury.

My personality, influenced by years of training from my parents to be pleasant and accommodating, provided an environment that muted my Mars to manifest polite boldness.

Practically, I had no other jobs lined up, so I had to be diplomatic. I did excellent work, but management was not going to be sidelined. Their will was going to be done. They would make it my business to promote their budding medical practice.

By the end of the week, Trixie and Vanessa presented me with an ultimatum cloaked as a partnership, a seeming boon, especially since I had worked there less than six months. It was an opportunity to own part of the empire as a partner. They told me that I had done well enough in the practice that they would exercise the option of offering me a partnership now, instead of after my first year of work. Offering me a partnership after I told them I wouldn't promote their business didn't make sense to me.

Management didn't give anything away, so I studied the contract over the weekend to see what the catch was. The document was tactfully clouded with legal language referring to me as an owner—if I signed on the dotted line.

Then, I came to the conclusion that employees would get regular salaries but as an owner and a stockholder, I would only get paid if we were profitable. Somehow, I knew there wouldn't be much profit. If I signed the contract, I would be working for free! Aha! They were trying to manipulate me into a situation where I would have no choice but to work harder in order to pay my bills.

They'd read me wrong. Intellectual Mercury was at work helping my analytic Virgo rising rationalize the situation. Lucky Jupiter was an ally in my sixth house of obstacles and struggles.

My parents always wanted me to have job security. I didn't want them to worry about my situation, so I didn't call to tell them what was happening. I called my friend Sunil, and he told me to consult my lawyer if I wanted to keep the job, or walk away. "If they're trying to screw you over now, think of how they'll be treating you in the future."

Obligations occupied my thoughts: school loans, food, lodging, and car payments. The contract didn't offer a steady income. This job wasn't worth fighting for. I would start making calls to a headhunter.

Vanessa was in the main office where I worked on Mondays. This was not a coincidence. She was hanging around making small talk. "How are things going?" she casually asked me.

Well, this was as good a time as any to get it over with. Softly, I answered her real question with a declaration: "I'm flattered at the opportunity to become a partner, but I'm not able to sign the contract. I need a regular income. I'm already working a lot of hours. I can't do more."

Visibly, she got two inches shorter as her lungs deflated upon hearing my unexpected refusal. Their trap hadn't worked. Her shoulders stooped and her facial expression flattened as she said, "Well, you've been working out so well." She didn't offer any compromise, or any other comments, other than "Okay," as she turned her back to continue with her duties.

We went back to our sterile employee-employer relationship. I returned to business as usual but with pride that I'd stood up for myself. But then again, I forgot that Vanessa wasn't the negotiator. Consequences weren't so obvious since I was new to the business frame of mind. All I knew was to take care of patients. Management was not done with me yet.

The next day, without ceremony, I was told by the accountant that I would be let go in two weeks. I didn't remember reading the clause in the partnership offer that if I didn't become partner, I would be terminated. Neither Trixie nor Vanessa was present to discuss this action. I felt it was another strategy. The unexpected dismissal was meant to unsettle me. It did. If I wanted my job, I would have to contact them and succumb to their conditions. But I didn't flinch.

They'd read me wrong.

After a half a second of confusion, I just said, "Okay," giving no thought to my financial obligations.

Aries lived in my eighth house of other people's money, representing the salary I wouldn't be making. Aries was symbolized by the ram, which by nature was bold and impulsive. Courageous Mars acted quickly and could make quick decisions.

But in the next few seconds, all I felt was relief. The universe answered. This past weekend, I no longer cared whether I lived close to my beloved beach. All I kept thinking was how would I make it through to the end of my yearly contract. I had six more months to go. I couldn't stand the predatory nature of the people who dictated my work environment.

I stayed quiet as the accountant, uncomfortable in the role of henchman, stammered while instructing me to return any company equipment, including office keys and mobile phone, by Friday of next week.

Later, thoughts of how bills were going to be paid preoccupied my mind, but I looked forward to a future free of this toxic environment. I needed a job, but I knew they needed me more. In less than two weeks, when I walked away, I only had myself to think of, but Vanessa had the burden of caring for all my patients as well as hers.

It wasn't the tragedy for me that they imagined.

The next Sunday I spent the day with my dad's cousin and her family. They lived in the neighboring town of Cape Coral across the Caloosahatchee River, just west of Fort Myers. Previously, I had given them sketchy details of my problems at work, minimizing the drama so as to keep the family gossip to a minimum. Now when I told my aunt that I was going to be leaving the practice, she encouraged me to come to church with the family.

I opted instead to swim in their pool. It was the end of February, and in full sun the temperature would hit the midseventies. Before I jumped in the water, my aunt, a devout Catholic, chided, "Don't you want God to help you?"

My well-rehearsed response to this question from various family members was a pious, "Don't you think He's helped me to get this far?"

My aunt's frown softened, and I imagined her thinking, *God has helped her.* Unable to give a more persuasive argument, she turned around without comment and headed to church.

I had an hour all to myself.

Floating on an inner tube, my thoughts quieted as I paddled the cool water with my feet and hands, moving from the shallow to the deep end and back, over and over. Mindlessly, I watched the occasional cloud pass over me. The warm sun felt good.

My religious background helped to form who I was. In the Philippines and in the United States, my parents enrolled their children in parochial schools. We read scripture and celebrated all the Christian holidays. We learned about the seven sacraments that imparted divine grace and strengthened faith. My parents initiated us into the Church with the sacraments of baptism and confirmation. When partaking of the sacrament of the Eucharist, we were blessed with the body and blood of Christ, the transformed wine and wafer. The healing sacraments were reconciliation (confession) and penance, and anointing of the sick. The sacrament of service, the holy orders was conferred on the clergy to spread the word of God. Learning the rules and structure of the Catholic Church gave me perspective.

I valued my Catholic background. The sermons taught lessons. The songs and rituals were joyous, hopeful, and full of mystery. I still believed in the Ten Commandments, but the institutional rules were no longer useful to me, and hadn't been for a long time. I still had faith, but not blind faith. I still considered myself to be a good Catholic, but I didn't conform to all the rules. My scientific education taught me to question, to reevaluate the rules and analyze them. If guidelines didn't make sense to me, I didn't follow them, and I learned not to feel guilty.

I grew up with the mindset of daily prayer and Sunday worship as a habit to weather any difficulty, but I'd stopped going to church a long time ago. In college, with no car and weekly service a five-mile walk from my dormitory, I rationalized that God would want me to sleep so that my mind would be sharp enough to pass tests so that I could become a doctor and heal people. After becoming an overworked physician, I justified that God would want me to rest so that I could be more effective in treating patients. After so many years, I'd come to the conclusion that I could still be a good person, spiritual—without going to church.

I hadn't been a strict Catholic since I left for college. On the rare occasion when I accompanied my parents to church, the priest reminded me—well, the congregation, though it felt as if the message was for my benefit—that only those whose sins have been absolved through the sacrament of confession were worthy to partake of the Holy Communion, the bread and wine transformed into the body and blood of Christ.

The analytic Virgo and the intellectual Mercury in me rationalized that He would consider the good person I strived to be and forgive me as I partook of the Communion, for those who receive it are brought to eternal life with our Lord in heaven. The tenets of the Catholic Church informed my decisions and my morality, but I could no longer follow all the rules blindly. The Bible described a vengeful but loving God, who forgave his people's indiscretions. I, too, was full of contradictions reflecting the characteristics of my God. He would forgive me.

I turned to prayer when facing difficulty, but I believed that He would forgive my choice to pray by myself in a swimming pool bathed in sunlight rather than with a congregation inside a concrete structure. I believed in the power of prayer to help in many situations, but I also believed that God helps those who help themselves. Relaxing in the warm sunshine was my way to think of a practical solution to my current job situation.

With my eyes closed, I noticed the faint, sweet smell of pine-apples. I'd smiled when my uncle described how when he sliced the crown of each pineapple, he would leave a little bit of fruit. He then would plop each crown on the ground outside the perimeter of the screened-in pool. "You don't even have to dig a hole to plant them, they grow so easily," he explained. Besides providing fruit, the plants surrounding the screened-in lanai were an added barrier to any wandering alligators or crocodiles headed in the direction of the pool. The Florida Everglades was the only place on Earth where both species coexist.

Conversation broke my reverie. My aunt and uncle were back with company. Eliza, the daughter of one of my aunt's friends, was with them, walking toward the pool. She was my age and was welcomed company. I'd met her about two months prior when my aunt hosted a holiday party.

Eliza and I stayed outside to talk by the pool while the rest of the family and guests ate inside. We hadn't known each other very long, but I was very comfortable with her. She was very open. When I first met her, she had introduced me to her son, who was about a foot taller than both of us. He was seventeen years old. When we were alone, I asked her, "You look like you're my age. When did you have Jeremy?"

She had been a teenage mother, getting pregnant at the age of sixteen. "My parents helped to raise him."

"Well, I think you did a good job. He seems so mature and polite. Do you have any other children?" I asked.

"He's the only one."

Over lunch she listened to my saga. I never mentioned an interest in the divination arts, but to my surprise Eliza told me that she'd consulted with a person at the flea market who was a psychic. "She's really helped me with problems I've had with my family." Although her parents were supportive, she had explained she'd had a complicated life.

"Well, how long have you been going to her?"

"I found her about six years ago. I thought I'd try her to see what she had to say. And since then, I've gone to her when I wanted some advice." My ears perked up hearing there was an intuitive in town. I wasn't sure, but I guessed Eliza continued to see her psychic since she got advice without judgment.

Eliza explained, "She also reads tarot cards, does numerology and some astrology. Why don't you go see Jacy?"

Before Eliza reached into her purse and pulled out a purple business card, I'd already decided to get a reading. I took the card thinking that even in a pool, prayer worked.

Chapter 10:

A Flea Market Find

The purple business card read: *Psychic Graphology, Tarot, Kirlian Photography, Numerology, Biorhythms, Astrology. Open Market Booth—Green 36.* At a flea market? An unusual office location, but Eliza promised, "She's good."

I was much more eager to see an intuitive than a priest. Both offered hope, but I wanted an alternative advisor who would offer guidance with anonymity. A priest would want to get to know me, and I'd be spending a lot of time explaining my situation. I wasn't looking for support or spirituality.

I booked a twenty-minute, twenty-dollar appointment later that afternoon before the flea market closed at 6 p.m. I was anxious to see what information the twenty minutes would yield to help me navigate my earthly path.

In ancient times, priests belonged to the upper class who devoted their life to education, including the study of the visible planets and the luminaries in the sky, the Sun and Moon. Through observation of planetary movements and the events on Earth, these priests came to the conclusion that the laws governing the movements of the celestial bodies were connected to the events on Earth. Cycles of the Moon were important for agriculture. Seasons changed with the path of the sun.

These priests were early astronomers responsible for picking auspicious times for celebration and rituals, such as sacrifice in the interest of their king and for the prosperity of their society. Except for the king, their priests weren't concerned with how the common man was affected by objects in the sky.

Because the celestial spheres perceptible to the naked eye were familiar considerations of daily life, observers began describing them as having human attributes. From a distance, the surface of Mars appeared reddish and became associated with the god of war. Venus, the brightest planet visible in the night sky, was considered the most beautiful and became associated with feminine allure. Endowed with human characteristics, these planetary gods would also be susceptible to being flattered with ceremonies to curry favor, such as for a good harvest or to appease wrath that manifested as inclement weather. The priest-astronomers were the mediators of these practices since they were knowledgeable about celestial behavior, the patterns made by the planets in the sky.

Their practice differed from that of contemporary astrologers who tend to specialize in forecasting for the individual. The duties of the modern clerical successors to these early priest-astronomers evolved to facilitating spiritual guidance and performing rites with no connections to the movement of the planets in the sky.

I wasn't seeking salvation as I drove to the flea market. I was hoping to get information on where I might get another job. The area was a field with covered tents housing separate booths. The smell of buttery popcorn, hot dogs, and hamburgers floated in the enclosed area. Bargain shoppers, window-shoppers, hagglers, and lost newbies, young and old and in between, crowded the maze of the flea market. The aisles were identified by different colors, and stalls were numbered to orient the visitors. The atmosphere was fun, with crystals and fabulous glittery costume jewelry mixed in with practical household items, sports memorabilia, and anything else that you could think of.

Normally, I would have stopped to examine every trinket, but it was hot and humid and I was anxious to glean any information about my future. Would this psychic/astrologer/tarot card reader/numerologist tell me anything that would help me?

I wandered to the "Open Market Booth, Green 36," earlier than my appointed time, curious to see what my Oracle of Delphi looked like and restless for my turn.

The booth entrance had a clear sliding door, which provided some privacy, allowing only muffled conversation to pass through the barrier. I peered in from the side of the stall pretending to look at the table of costume jewelry positioned outside the office. The appointment sheet hanging on the glass partition indicated that the current client had ten minutes more before my turn.

I watched as Jacy stood up to signal the close of the session. She was a tall brunette with straight hair past her shoulders and wore candy apple–red reading glasses.

A chime attached to the sliding door tinkled, signaling the opening and closing of the partition. Before Jacy slid the door closed, we greeted each other.

"You're right on time. Sit down," she said with a cheerful voice, directing me to sit on the white plastic lawn chair closest to the entrance. Sheer white curtains covered the panels of the stall. Sunlight diffused through the canvas roof giving a glow to the interior of the booth, and a small fan cooled the quartered space.

On the round table in front of me was a pen, a pad of paper, a deck of tarot cards, and a tape recorder. Jacy sat across from me, sandwiched on either side by pictures of pastel-colored angels that hung on the wall behind her. I wondered if these otherworldly creatures were guides or just for ambience.

She spoke with a slow drawl, enunciating her words authoritatively. She explained that she'd be doing calculations for the numerology part of the reading and asked me for my birth data.

Once done with her computation, she clicked the timer on and my twenty minutes started. She instructed me to lay my hands on the table, palms up. Then, she placed her palms over mine for a few seconds and explained, "I like to physically connect with my client's energy. That's why I don't do phone readings."

Pointing to the pen and paper on my side of the table, she said, "Write anything. Just a few sentences. I just want to see how you write." She took what I wrote, turned on the tape recorder, and started her analysis.

"When the left side lines up, you'll learn to handle money," she said, pointing to the left-hand margins of my paragraph that sloped downward and to the right.

"Well, right now I have no money to handle," I confessed.

"Pay attention to lining up the left margins, and you'll do better with money."

"Okay," I consented. It wasn't much to ask.

Next was numerology. She turned the piece of paper so I could see the numbers she was pointing to and then began: "Alright, now you're in a pinnacle of change and the unexpected. You have two numbers alike, double fives, and it can cause a negative reaction. You have two change cycles. So, it's either going to be chaotic or mellow or a combination. Has it been crazy this year?"

"Very crazy," I replied.

"Your life goes smoothly and then, all of a sudden, it kinda changes out of nowhere. Okay. You're in kind of a lull right now. It's about time for everything to start changing. Last year you made new starts and new beginnings in a lot of different areas. This year you can fall in love or end either a relationship or a job. Something major. I have a feeling, maybe, you should be in another place also. I don't know." The psychic part was coming out. "I don't feel that you're a troublemaker, but I'm picking up some of the dog-eat-dog situation with everybody else around you. It's hard to live with."

"I'm not in a good work environment. I took a job where I kept being assigned more and more work. I complained and was let go."

Jacy was transitioning to different modalities seamlessly, her dialogue continuing uninterrupted.

Next came the tarot card reading. The colorful cards had symbols of cups, swords, and different characters whose meaning was based on her interpretation and my energy. She asked me to shuffle the deck and spread them out facedown in a semicircle and to pick ten cards. She turned the cards over in the order I chose them and started explaining their significance. "Okay. Someone is gonna tell you about an opening, but I don't know if it's open yet, an upcoming opening, workwise. In two days, two weeks, or two months, you will get another job. You will have whatever funds you need to relocate. Don't worry," she reassured me.

"My last day is this Friday, so my job will end this week." I hoped she was right about the job opening, but I also thought that what she was saying was too good to be true because it was so exact.

"You can fit in nicely wherever you go. Pick another card." I kept picking cards until she turned the whole deck over. A mantra in my head kept repeating: *two days, two weeks, or two months.*

All too soon, her timer started beeping, signaling five minutes left to go. With the last card, she said, "Okay, you're a little lonely, but you're so busy that you don't really think about it too much. Right now, you gotta get your career going. And I know that you can work anywhere. Just put some résumés out. The number two keeps coming up. You're going to get another job in *two* days, *two* weeks, or *two* months. Start sending out résumés."

I came out of the reading hopeful, just like after Sam's reading. Sam had predicted I would be in a job by the fall of 1995, which happened. He said by January, I would travel over water, and over the Christmas holidays I traveled to India.

Jacy got my current work situation right. It had been a crazy year: finishing training in Milwaukee, working for one week in Maine, starting and ending a Florida job in six months. And now, another job in two days, two weeks, or two months. Would she be right about this too? I would know soon enough.

Right now, all I could do was finish out a busy week and after that, sort things out, and start looking for a new job.

The previous summer, I'd contacted Ruth, a colleague of mine from residency training in New York, just to keep in touch. She worked at the Veterans Hospital in Miami. I let her know that I'd be working in Fort Myers in the fall. In the week after my reading with Jacy, Ruth called. She was working at the Miami Veterans Administration Medical Center. One of the doctors in the department was retiring. If I interviewed, the job would be mine. I interviewed, and *two* weeks after my reading with Jacy, I was offered a new job.

Wow! Sam's prediction also came to mind. When Magda and I saw him last March, he'd asked, "Have you ever worked for a city, state, or gov'ment? You work for 'em now? Because there's a step coming, and I'll still go with May or June. They're changin' somethin' that'll give you an opportunity." Now, less than one year later, what he described was coming to pass. Instead of May or June of 1995, it would be in March of 1996 that the "opportunity" would open up. Sam did say that he wasn't sure of the timing.

Last year, Sam's reading was confusing since he described that I would have several jobs. I never imagined that I would be changing jobs as often as I had in the past eleven months since that appointment. At the time, Sam's description of my future opportunities was just a jumble of possibilities with no clear direction, but in fact, his predictions reflected what I had gone through and was still going through.

The lawyer I hired to protect my legal interests during contract negotiation for my Fort Myers job included a clause to give me severance pay. It was enough to pay for a deposit and first and last month's rent on an apartment in Miami.

Jacy said, "In two days, two weeks, or two months, you will get another job. You will have whatever funds you need to relocate. Don't worry."

How did she know?

Chapter 11:

Sightseeing in Miami, 1997

I started my new job at the Miami Veterans Administration Medical Center within one month of my reading with Jacy. I was in a state of disbelief even as I experienced the manifestation of her predictions. I've encountered enough intuitives to know that the phenomenon of foresight occurs, but to have the circumstances come to pass so accurately and immediately was confounding.

Sam and Jacy foretold outcomes in the absence of prior knowledge. They asked specific questions to see if what they saw or thought matched my situation, but I didn't give them any detailed accounting of my past to point them in any specific direction. In my twenty-to-thirty-minute appointments, they were able to receive information crossing unseen boundaries of communication and time.

As a doctor, I could reasonably predict the path of disease. I could provide scenarios on possible medical outcomes based on data. I asked patients questions about their medical and social histories. Facts, such as a person's family history, and habits, like food choices and exercise regime, allowed me to formulate opinions about the cause of their symptoms and their tendencies for health-related problems, like heart disease, diabetes, and even risk for cancer. This interaction focused my physical examination and treatment plan. I was limited in my prediction skills. My prognosis for a patient's health condition consisted of possible outcomes within a range dictated by their history and lab data.

Modern science taught me that almost every effect had a likely cause and that whatever wasn't obvious could be clarified by advanced medical technology, by evaluating body fluids or by radiographic means. Disease could manifest with or without unhealthy physical habits depending on genetic predisposition. Environment and medications could modify disease. That was a cause-and-effect relationship that I could understand.

Both Sam and Jacy had perceptions they could translate as being separate from themselves and associated with my future. Sam interpreted vibrations with the help of his spirit guide, Sweet Willow. He characterized his reading as only possibilities, though some of his predictions came to pass. Jacy physically connected with my energy by placing her palms over mine, but this link didn't explain how her forecast was so specific.

I didn't know how to learn the psychic skills of prediction that Sam and Jacy had. That was why I was drawn to studying astrology; the subject had concepts and tangible rules that could be learned.

Each time I went to see an intuitive, I got some clarity regarding my life's circumstances. I would observe the practitioners to get clues about their techniques but didn't have time to interview them as to how they developed their abilities. I believed that Sam and Jacy's abilities were genuine, and my scientific side kept telling me there was a rationale to explain their skills, I just hadn't found it yet.

I was busy trying to establish a medical practice, so my questions had to be placed on a back burner, when I had more time. I laughed while thinking that the research would have to be done on my own dime. I doubted that the National Institute of Health would grant me funding to research what the future held for me.

Once I found Iris, I was a regular attendee of her intermittent Saturday astrology workshops. I learned the basic terminology, what the planets and the different sections of the astrological wheel meant. To help our class learn how to interpret an astrological chart, Iris used our charts as examples.

I applied the tenets of astrology like layers of paint onto the canvas of who I was. The horoscopic chart was an astrological representation of my tendencies and characteristics. It was another way to describe myself. My actions were reflected in my horoscope. As I learned more and more about myself, I discovered my self-portrait wasn't a classic masterpiece painting but a caricature, colorful and distorted with exaggerated peculiarities. It was a way to view my strengths and weakness objectively. I found myself and the process to be very interesting.

The ninth house played a major role in my chart. It described the exaggerated influences in my life. My preconceived ideas of higher education and teachers was the traditional university route, but they had become more inclusive as curious Mercury began to explore advisors who were able to access information through unconventional techniques. Mercury lived with the life-giving Sun, who allowed my interests to grow. My aggressive soldier, Mars, was non-traditional and lived in the eighth house of transformation, in his own sign of Aries. He was an educational warrior with his aggression directed to seeking knowledge from all sorts of teachers, from university professors to psychics, mediums, astrologers, and tarot card readers. My medical occupation was in the sixth house of service and its tenant, lucky Jupiter, helped me overcome obstacles, like rigorous medical training, and made sure I was never without a job. I was living my chart.

Saturn was also strong in my chart. He lived in the fifth house, in the sign of Capricorn that he owned, so he was very comfortable being himself with all that his house represented, taking responsibility and having the discipline to learn from the obstacles of life. The fifth house signifies the higher mind (intelligence), romance, and creativity. It represents children as the expression of creativity (procreation) as well as the inner child who wants to play and enjoy life. The mountain goat is the symbol of Capricorn, persistent, disciplined, headstrong, and focused to its lofty goals, such as climbing to the top of the mountain. I got a double dose of discipline and sense of obligation, with Saturn in the sign of Capricorn. Saturn is the disciplinarian of the planets in our solar system. Before the outer planets (planets located beyond Saturn) were discovered, Saturn was the outermost planet that could be seen by the naked eye. Neptune was discovered on September 23, 1846, and Pluto on February 18, 1930. Saturn represented a boundary, the limitations of the planets. In astrology, Saturn is a hard teacher who provides obstacles for the person, lessons to learn in life. By overcoming hurdles, the individual reaps the benefits from the education provided by Saturn.

Discipline and obligation to duty are strong qualities in my constitution. After college, I studied for nine more years. I stayed with the study of medicine throughout my New York experience and overcame all the challenges that the field of medicine could throw at a doctor. I made sure I could provide for myself, and this self-reliance allowed me the freedom to explore my interests.

When you are young, your family is your environment. The environmental influence strengthened my discipline by example from my parents. Dad immigrated from the Philippines to the United States in 1967 to improve our family circumstances. By 1969, he had saved enough to bring my mother and the remaining children to America. By changing our environment, he changed his family's future possibilities.

In the Philippines, my mother owned and operated a corner grocery store. In the new world, she secured a job as a registered nurse at a local hospital where we settled in Gary, Indiana. When my mom was sixteen, my grandmother lied about her age, saying she was eighteen so that she could get into nursing school. She eventually worked as a nurse during World War II.

In Gary, Mom worked a forty-hour workweek from 3–11 p.m. She got home around midnight or 1 a.m. and was up again at 6 a.m. to make the family breakfast before sending us kids to school and seeing my father off to work. She then went to sleep. Before going back to work, she cooked dinner, which was ready for us when we got home from school.

Mom rarely complained about any daily routine, but one weekend morning, after five years of the above schedule, she started yelling at my father. My dad was on his way out to play tennis with my brothers. She was tired of doing laundry by hand for her family, a husband and three sons who played tennis every day, as well as two daughters. I never did the wash, but my sister and I would hang the clothes to dry in the backyard and fold them afterwards. Dad also worked hard but was oblivious as to how my mother ran the household. Dad's role was to be the breadwinner. Care of the home was Mom's responsibility. In the Philippines, we had domestic help to do all the household chores. Dad didn't realize all the work Mom did until she spoke up. That day, he didn't take my brothers to play tennis. He took my mom to Sears and bought a washer and dryer.

The Sun represents a father figure, strength and authority. In my chart, the Sun lives in the ninth house and strongly encourages education. My mother, the nurturer, represented by the Moon, lives in the tenth house, in the sign of Gemini. She showed me strength in the career roles she had as a nurse and mother.

The parents' influence can be seen in a child's horoscopic chart much like the parents' genetic material can be observed in the physical (phenotype) and personality characteristics of their child. Iris told us that when studying charts of family members, she saw patterns that interconnected their horoscopic information. It made me wonder if planetary configurations were inherited like genetic material.

I learned to take responsibility for the people who depended on me. I learned to work hard and persist in accomplishing what needed to be done. I learned not to complain about hard work. From watching my parents' examples of responsibility, my character developed.

It had been five years since my internship in New York City, and I just hit the jackpot. I was in Miami. I lived close enough to the beach to hear the sound of the waves. Every time I felt the ocean breeze, I couldn't help but take it all in with deep breaths. It was heaven. My job at the Veterans Administration Medical Center allowed me to practice medicine and pursue topics that were becoming more than a hobby.

The city of Miami was more like a foreign country than a city within the geographic limits of the United States. The Latin influence was everywhere. Even in the grocery stores, use of the Spanish language was common. Some of the cashiers didn't hesitate to show their irritation when I asked them to repeat themselves in English.

When my father came to visit, I took him to Ocean Drive in South Beach. We people-watched, walking past the outdoor restaurants on one side, with the ocean on the other. Dad surprised me when he remarked in a heavy, staccato Filipino accent, "God sakes! Der arrh so meny furenhers here."

I looked at Dad to see if he was joking. He wasn't. I said nothing. *People probably think you're the foreigner,* I thought. Many people hailed from the Caribbean Islands and South America because Miami was easily accessible, in close proximity to their country, and was a fun city.

Fort Myers was a distant memory. I now had free time. Living close to the beach created the atmosphere of a working vacation. I was able to enjoy the ocean when not at work. I also noticed more advertisements announcing psychics and psychic fairs in the paper and pinned to grocery store bulletin boards. Flyers advertising Selena the Psychic would appear on the windshield of my parked car. Research material. I could explore.

I took my time and read the notices promising knowledge of where and when I would meet my "soul mate," and those that gave hope about the bounty that tomorrow might hold. Given the opportunity, who wouldn't want to bypass any unpleasantness in their life?

I developed a practiced list of investigation criteria once I got to my face-to-face appointment: letting the individual do most of the talking, avoiding buying any talisman to attract a mate or promote good luck and prosperity—no matter how attractive the promise of reward—and no exchange of money for rituals to appease the spirits or gain their favor.

Psychic fairs were perfect venues for my research. The crowds were eclectic and so were the practitioners. It was easy to see which practitioners had empty seats and those who had a waiting list. I could observe who projected the most sincerity and which were performers.

Street fairs provided opportunities to eavesdrop discreetly. With the stalls so close together, I would pretend to compare the merits of a four-hundred-thread-count bedsheet with that of an eight-hundred-count while listening to a reading less than five feet away.

Was the practitioner a psychic, an astrologer, a palm or tarot card reader, a channeler of spirit energies, or a combination? Was the intuitive cajoling or intense as she gave advice to a young girl just dumped by her boyfriend? Who was doing most of the talking when a client came to ask for direction in his life?

The more upscale Lincoln Road in South Beach was a great

place to wander. It had many sidewalk cafés and funky stores but was a more discreet locale. Fortune-tellers were present in the evenings. There usually were only one or two in the whole area between popular restaurants, so it was not so easy to eavesdrop. After casually walking by more than two or three times, I would get noticed.

In the evenings, the crowd was more couples-oriented. Love and romance were in the air. Combined with the balmy weather, the setting was perfect to support the feeling that hopes and dreams could come true.

The seers intentionally cultivated a look of being from some exotic and mysterious culture. Most had an ethnic accent or feigned one. Swarthy men were simply attired, wearing white shirts and dark pants, while the women were more flamboyant, accessorized, and dressed in flowing skirts and scarves.

The setup was simple, often just two chairs and a round, folding table, perhaps with flowers for decoration. Colorful cards would be used during the reading as a focal point for the reader or as a distraction for the client. Most times, some sort of crystal added sparkle during the evening hours. Candlelight reinforced the aura of mysticism.

If their chair was vacant, the soothsayer would call out to the passersby hoping to make eye contact with a curious onlooker who had anticipation in their eyes—or better yet, a couple with hope in their hearts. "Do you want to know your future? Come, I will tell you."

I wasn't drawn to any of them.

With each deep inhalation, facing the ocean on Miami Beach, I felt freedom fill my lungs. I settled into a seated, cross-legged yoga pose. With the ocean breeze washing over me, my eyes closed, and my breathing in sync with the waves coming to shore, I remembered the stressful circumstances of my journey to get here: the challenges of becoming a doctor, the fear of getting HIV, the frustration in Fort Myers. I slowly let them go with each exhalation to disappear with the setting sun.

We all met because of a sign: "Yoga on the beach, 6 p.m." Monroe, who'd recently lost a ton of weight, was the former public relations man for a well-known former big-city mayor and now a beach-yoga instructor. Fiona and Alice, an entrepreneurial couple who often vacationed in Miami Beach, were now permanent transplants from New Jersey. Jonathan, tall and Adonis-looking, was a New York City financial broker turned restaurateur, and Myrna, a dentist also from the New York City area, was recently married and looking for a new start. We were all searching for something else.

It was on that beach where I learned about Iris. Fiona told me, "I go to her every year to get business advice and ask about people I know." Fiona consulted with this psychic astrologer for years, to get the lay of the land about what she could expect for the immediate future. She asked about different job and investment prospects, whether business and personal relationships were viable or not, and even about the timing of certain activities. Fiona described Iris as an intuitive who seemed to be able to answer practical and specific questions on a regular basis.

What Fiona described was like an annual health exam with a family doctor to ensure a healthy and productive life, but with an intuitive. As a physician, a yearly checkup made sense to me, but with regard to a psychic who was an astrologer? This, I had to check out.

"Iris has weekly demonstrations," Fiona volunteered.

The next Wednesday night, Fiona, Alice, Myrna, and I entered a North Miami office building at 7:00 p.m. for Iris's weekly demonstration. When we reached the front of the line, Fiona greeted Étienne, who was seated behind a desk at the entrance of the conference room collecting the twenty-five-dollar fee. "How are you? I haven't seen you for a while."

Étienne, red-haired and freckled, replied, "Nice to see you," and moved us along the line after handing each of us a piece of paper with a list of planets next to blank lines for our first name and date, time, and place of birth. "Write down your birth information. When you're done, give it to Stacey, and she'll fill out the rest," she said, pointing to the person seated next to her. "Then take a seat. Iris will be in around seven thirty."

Fiona oriented us, explaining that Étienne was Iris's assistant and Stacey was Iris's daughter. Fiona told us, "Stacey's gonna give us back that sheet describing where the planets were located at the time of our birth. Iris needs that to do the astrology."

"Where does she get that information?" I asked.

Fiona pointed to a paperback book with a red cover that Stacey had in front of her. "That book is an ephemeris. It catalogues the position of the planets, Sun, and Moon as they move throughout the day. She looks up the year and time you were born and lists where the planets were positioned on your birthday."

"So, she creates the horoscope too?" Myrna asked.

Fiona looked at us and said, "Iris will ask you to read your list of planets, and Étienne will draw the chart on the board. Iris's good. You'll see."

"Really? Is Iris gonna get to all of us?" I asked. I'd never been to a psychic demonstration like this before. I wasn't sure how Iris was going to read more than one horoscope at a time, accurately, without preparation to analyze the chart.

Fiona took the lead in choosing seats. "Let's try to get close to the front. We'll have a better chance of being read." The room was packed with what looked like forty folding chairs. I already counted ten other attendees besides us. I was getting irritated because I didn't want to compete to get a reading. We got four seats together in front, just to the left of a dry-erase board and an armchair where I assumed Iris would be seated.

I looked back toward the entrance and saw Stacey heading in our direction. She was polite and sociable as she handed out our planetary information. I searched her face to see if there were clues, if she had some different qualities due to having a mother who was a psychic astrologer. But there was nothing out of the ordinary, just a friendly smile and slightly bulging eyes, framed by a dark-blonde bob.

By the sound of the conversation around me, I determined that the people present were either repeat visitors or accompanied by repeat visitors. They came with questions: "I want to know if this house in Coral Gables is a good investment." Or, "I'm asking about my mom's health." I could understand a little Spanish and gleaned that the couple behind me were going to ask about their immigration status. Did Iris speak Spanish? I guessed I'd find out if they got called. A comment one friend said to another caught my attention: "If she calls on me, please write down what she says, and I'll do the same for you."

Ever ready, I took out my notebook and pen, turned to Myrna, and asked her to write down whatever Iris had to say if I got picked. I would do the same for her, Fiona, and Alice.

Myrna was nearing forty and wanted a career change after ten years of dentistry. Fiona and Alice wanted to start a massage therapy business and were looking for a good date to open their doors. Moving to Miami had already brightened my future. Of course, I was interested in any information about my life, but I was also interested in Iris's process. Most of all, I was excited not to have to skulk around and eavesdrop to observe her process like I'd done at the street fairs.

I turned around when I heard a shuffling noise by the door. Fiona whispered, "She's here." Iris looked to be in her mid to late sixties, with shoulder-length jet-black hair and bulging eyes, more prominent than Stacey's. If she'd had a pointed hat and broom to go with her black top and pants, she could've passed for a carica-ture of a witch. She greeted acquaintances as she entered, making her way to the seat in front. Her ready smile and friendly manner dispelled my image of a sorcerer.

She scanned the room and acknowledged familiar faces as she took her seat. In a hoarse New York accent, Iris began, "Hi, everyone." She pointed to the dry-erase board and said, "Étienne listed where the planets are located today. And you got a list of where their position was on the day you were born. The Moon is the closest planet to Earth, so it affects us more. It changes zodiac sign every two and a half days. It represents the subconscious, our emotions, what we can't see."

She got right to teaching, which I liked. Good. I didn't think I was coming to a lecture, but I was excited to see how she worked. I was ready to take notes. I could make sense of what I didn't understand later.

"The Moon's not really a planet but Earth's satellite. It's a luminary, like the Sun. They both give off light, but the Moon shines from the reflected rays of the Sun. The Sun gives power to the area of the chart where it resides. Nothing grows without the Sun. It stays in one sign for thirty to thirty-one days. The Sun represents what's obvious about a person, the outward appearance. You gave Étienne the time you were born. Some people don't know the exact time, but it makes a difference. Your rising sign, the constellation rising in the east at the time you were born, represents your personality, your likes and dislikes. It's who you really are. It can be different from your outward appearance. You all know people who act different from what they look like."

Her monologue continued as she explained a few more things to us: "This is how I get my brain in a different state. I'm winding up the motor by my constant talking. *Rrrrr, rrrrr,* I look like I'm wide-awake talking to you, but I'm going into a different state. I'm opening up my third eye. I can see better with the pineal gland than with two eyes. When I go home, I close the pineal gland and open my two eyes—that's when I go blind." I guessed she meant once she could see with her physical vision, her psychic vision shut down.

I often arrived at work by 7 a.m., and it was already past my bedtime. While her droning voice put her in a heightened state of awareness, the continuous hum was lulling me to sleep. I was determined to stay until the end to witness her readings. To conserve my energy, I limited the visual stimuli, opening my eyes only to write notes. Taking deep breaths, I was able to keep awake and concentrate on her words, which flowed to my right hand.

"The third eye is associated with the pineal gland in our brain. The pineal gland secretes hormones that regulate our body rhythms. As we get older, the pineal gland dries up if we don't use it. I'm exercising this organ like a muscle by practicing my intuition. If you don't, it dries up and becomes calcified."

I opened my eyes upon hearing a medical term. I knew that the pineal gland, a pea-shaped organ that secretes the hormone melatonin, regulates our circadian rhythms, or sleep/wake cycles. The gland also converts the neurotransmitter serotonin into melatonin. Serotonin regulates mood, social behavior, appetite, digestion, sleep, memory, and sexual desire and function. Melatonin is a hormone used to help with insomnia.

Iris was accurate when she pointed to its placement, just above and between our eyebrows, in the center where the two hemispheres of the brain meet. The gland has cells with the same features as the light-sensitive cells in the retina of the eyes with connection to the visual cortex of the brain that processes images. Its location between the two halves of the brain allows access to information from both sides. So, the pineal gland influences the level of awareness and how the visual sense can be formed, perceived, and interpreted. This was the first time I was connecting with some sort of viable explanation for psychic ability.

Iris's voice continued in a steady hum, with little variation in tone. It was like white noise, which had a tendency to relax me. I had to take deep breaths to stop from nodding off. I was determined to stay awake when she read people. "The left brain is the logical side, representing astrology, and the right is creative, representing psychic ability. When I work, I'm using both at the same time. I see pictures in people's auras, and I experience it like a vocal close-captioned movie for the blind. When I read people, it's their movies, their story that I'm observing."

Could this be a learned skill? In an example of a more familiar sense of awareness, some people can feel the change in their body when their sugar level is low. They get irritable or weak and they know they have to eat something. If this was a skill, Iris was practicing at a significantly higher level of consciousness.

Hypnosis is a state of consciousness in which a person becomes responsive to suggestion or direction. Iris still had voluntary actions. She was able to direct Étienne to write on the dry-erase board. She asked and answered questions. No one was telling her what to do, so this wasn't strictly hypnosis. What Iris described seemed to be self-hypnosis to get into a different state of mind.

As an explanation of her process, she gave us some backstory: "I learned astrology first from Evangeline Adams's only disciple. Mrs. Stevens then brought out my psychic ability. In these demonstrations, I tell you what I see and then use astrology to confirm it. I first heard about Evangeline Adams when I lived in New York City. I wished I could've studied under her, but she lived in the late 1800s and early 1900s. The financier J. P. Morgan was one of Evangeline Adams's clients. He had the ceiling of the Morgan Library & Museum decorated with zodiac signs arranged in ways that were meaningful to him. If you get a chance, you should visit the museum."

It's another New York experience I'd missed. My coffee, now cold, continued to help keep me awake. Iris took no breaks.

As if reading my mind, she said, "In this state, I can't eat or drink anything. I'll choke. I'm not awake in the usual sense, and I'm not sleeping. When I first came to Miami in the 1960s, a group of us would meet in my house and I would start giving readings. Then, more and more people started showing up, and my husband told me he wanted his home back, and that I needed to find somewhere else. I found a place on Miami Beach. We were there for a while. After there was a fire, we had to find another place to hold these demonstrations. My demonstrations are my research laboratory. People come from different backgrounds and bring a variety of situations for me to analyze. I can test if I'm accurate. You all are the witnesses. I'm a Virgo with Scorpio rising. Virgo is the critic of the zodiac. Virgo digs and analyzes. I pick situations apart. I ask, why? Scorpio dissects information like a surgeon. Both can describe a psychic surgeon."

She'd been talking for over an hour and a half. I was getting impatient because I was fighting sleepiness. I didn't want to nod off when she got to reading people. That was what I was waiting for. How long was she going to take to warm up? While she got more alert during her monologue, her humming voice was lulling me to sleep. I looked around and no one had left. I stayed awake but had a hard time retaining the unfamiliar astrological concepts. I hoped my notes would make some sense when I reviewed them.

"An individual's personality is a reflection of the planet's nature." She gave an example of how Mercury, the planet of communication, would act in the different signs. "This is how a person born in the sign of Leo, the showman of the zodiac, would describe a car accident. If his Mercury was in the constellation of Taurus at the time of birth, this person would talk about the damage done to the car. If the planet was in Pisces, he would ask if anybody got hurt. Mercury in Virgo would want to know all the details of the event. With Mercury in the sign of Capricorn, the Leo person would be all business and ask whether the parties had insurance. With Mercury placed in the sign of Aquarius, representing the humanitarian, he would ask about the welfare of those involved. The Leo person with an Aries Mercury would impatiently describe the collision, while the Gemini Mercury would report it immediately."

It was after 9 p.m. when Iris started doing readings. Her informative rambling wasn't as aimless as it seemed. She started talking about how difficult relationships were for young people these days. Then she looked at a woman who appeared to be in her early twenties and asked her to read where the planets were listed on her sheet. Iris said she saw pictures, like a movie around a person's aura, when she read them. I wondered what she saw when she chose to read this client.

This young woman had come to inquire about her current relationship. Where would it lead? At first, she was open about her situation, then squirmed, getting uncomfortable as Iris mentioned complications with this affair. "Is there someone else involved?" she asked. After a little pressing, it came out that the man she hoped would be part of her future was married.

By asking questions, Iris was able to get confirmation of who she was reading. Inquiries ranged from family relationships, jobs, habits, and places where people lived. She seemed to be able to fast-forward or rewind events to focus on audience members' questions. When the person being read couldn't remember a date of an event or didn't know if her mom had been married to someone else before her dad, she would move the reading along by saying, "Write it down. Look at it later. That's what happens when people come into my energy. They get sleepy with my voice going *rrrr rrrr* and can't remember."

It was certainly happening to me, even with years of practice note-taking while being sleepy. But I'd always "written it down."

A returning attendee explained that she couldn't open her children's clothing business on the date Iris had given her a couple weeks ago. Could she get another date? Iris asked what date she'd been given, and the woman kept talking about why another time had to be chosen.

"Don't interrupt me. You're gonna stop your reading. It looks like I'm having a conversation with you, but if you keep talking, it takes me to my left brain and I have to be logical. You're interrupting the flow of your movie. Give me short answers. Okay, I'll give you another date, but it won't be as good."

For Myrna, Iris saw a new opportunity in the dental field but not as a clinician. Iris asked her if she had children, and Myrna revealed that she and her husband were trying to get pregnant. Fiona and Alice were given a date to ensure success of their business. Iris told the class, "The day you open your doors is the birthday of your business." For me, she saw that I moved a lot in my life. "You will have many more moves," she said.

Just after 2:30 a.m., Iris closed the demonstration by asking Étienne the time. "I have to sit here for a while and let my left brain take over. I can't be driving home in a dreamy state." She welcomed conversation with the straggling attendees who took one last opportunity to ask her questions. The interaction allowed transition to her logical side.

I was excited about the night's experience but was more tired. All I wanted to do was get home and catch a few hours of sleep before I had to be at the hospital. I would sort out the events of the evening later.

The next day, I focused on work to finish my obligations early and get home. Even with little sleep, I worked best in the mornings, a carryover from medical training. Fatigue would set in by early afternoon.

It was efficient to make rounds early, checking in with patients before they got out of bed, before the nurses got them ready for breakfast, therapies, or other scheduled tests. That way I wouldn't have to go looking for them. As a rehabilitation specialist, I took over patient care after their acute medical conditions were stabilized. The rehab team included nursing staff, social workers, psychologists, kinesiologists, and speech, recreation, physical, and occupational therapists. Our unit optimized the functional levels of debilitated patients with various diagnoses, including cancer, heart attacks, strokes, and amputations.

I was pleasantly surprised at how easily I settled into a

comfortable routine at work. Once the inpatient care was addressed, I directed my attention to the scheduled outpatient clinic, staff, and family meetings.

It was only when I took a thirty-minute lunch break that I thought about my Iris experience. I sat in my office going over the events of the past evening. Iris read about ten people that night. One after the other. When chosen, we read aloud the location of the list of planets Stacey gave us. Étienne then drew the circular astrological chart on the dry-erase board, placing the planets in their assigned sections. Iris did no preparation other than her monologue. With this information, she gave us accurate details about our lives. The experience was amazing. I had been tired but stayed awake during the whole process. I guessed that she could do some type of self-hypnosis to stimulate other parts of her brain. Her monologue had affected me, putting me in an altered state by making me sleepy. I had to fight to keep awake.

Iris described seeing pictures as movies in our auras. In the crowded room, she asked questions to differentiate one person's "movie" from another. She gave accurate readings consecutively, transitioning from one person to another for five hours straight.

Discussion of the pineal gland as the third eye showed her curiosity about the mechanism of her psychic abilities. She explained how she started out by learning astrology and then became more intuitive. Perhaps I could do that. I could learn the astrology, but I wasn't sure about the psychic ability.

There had to be some genetic predisposition for certain talents or insight. Sam could communicate with his spirit guide. Besides working with tarot cards, palmistry, and numerology, Jacy also had some psychic skills. Intuitive specialties. Hmm.

In past readings, I wondered how the practitioners were able to make suggestions for the future. How did they separate their information from that of their client? Eventually, I started looking at them as possible teachers, but most didn't give the impression of wanting to teach their craft. But really, I hadn't asked since I was busy getting established with my medical career. Iris was the first practitioner from whom I felt I could learn. She must be amenable to teaching. Didn't she spend seven hours a week doing demonstrations? She would understand my curiosity.

I sat in my office and opened the notebook from the previous night to the page where I wrote what she said about me. "You will have many more moves." It just hit me. I got sad thinking I wasn't going to be staying in my dream home by the beach. I got even more tired than I already was from my late night. I just sat back in my chair, my eyes closed with a heavy heart thinking I was going to be starting all over again. Then, I fell asleep.

When I woke up, I got energized with the thought that I have free will. What Iris says doesn't have to happen.

The rest of the workday was routine. My work got done without any emergencies or unplanned meetings. I got home before sunset and immediately got ready for my after-work routine. Yoga on the Beach met Tuesdays and Thursdays, so the other days I walked along the shoreline. My building on Collins Avenue was right on the Atlantic Ocean. I made a beeline to where the sand greeted the incoming tide. When I walked, I liked to feel the wet sand squishing between my toes. The warm, humid ocean breeze washing over me and the rhythmic sound of the waves uncluttered my mind, and my thoughts drifted to the events of the past evening.

As I made my way back to my apartment, I made a decision to study astrology.

Chapter 12:

The Reading

In Miami, my job was ideal. It was as close to a 9 to 5 workday that a physician could get and still feel comfortable that patients had twenty-four-hour coverage for any medical condition. The Veterans Hospital allowed me to balance medical work with a life away from the hospital.

In the study of any medical field, there are always newer and more efficient ways to treat patients. Practitioners have an obligation to update themselves with the current standards of care. Medical practitioners are always learning. This was the first time I felt that I was truly done with the formal process of medical training and could practice my profession. And I had time to relax. But true to my ninth house of higher learning, after several months of getting settled in my new home and job, I spent my time exploring another subject: astrology.

Iris held workshops in the same location where she did demonstrations but scheduled at a more reasonable mid-morning hour. Classes were structured like her demonstration sessions. She started with the planetary weather, where the planets were located on that day, followed by a monologue about different topics, including discussion of current events relative to the planetary placement. Similar to her demonstrations, anyone could attend. There were no prerequisites.

The lessons built on each other. We started with the zodiacal terms and their assigned relationship to nature. Étienne listed the astrological signs in groups. Iris stood up from her chair and pointed to the eraser board. "Fire signs are Aries, Leo, and Sagittarius. Air signs are Libra, Aquarius, and Gemini. Water signs are Cancer, Scorpio, and Pisces. Earth signs are Capricorn, Taurus, and Virgo. The characteristics of fire, air, water, and earth describe certain aspects of the signs, and the mixing of these four elements of nature can also describe man's nature. What I suggest is that you all start a binder and make twelve divisions for the twelve zodiac signs. When you learn something about Leo, then put it in the Leo section. When you learn something about Aries, put it in the Aries section. That way if you want to know about a sign, you can just flip to the section. A lot of people never do it, but I tell them anyway."

I had collections of notes that never got organized, and eventually the information got lost in piles of paper. The best way I'd found to catalogue information was to just use one notebook at a time. It was easier for me to find what I needed.

In the first classes I attended, Iris started with her monologue, shorter than during her demonstration, lasting about thirty minutes. "The Sun is the marker of the seasons as it makes its yearly journey across the constellations. The signs, named for the constellations, are described as cardinal, mutable, and fixed, and correspond to different aspects of each season."

Iris got up from her seat and started writing which signs were cardinal, mutable, and fixed. I wondered if she was in her altered state. Iris walked around as she moved in the semicircle of seated students. As she continued to describe the basic terms, she made eye contact with each of us. Iris's eyes bulged. I recognized it as a sign of an overactive thyroid. I couldn't help but imagine that she saw the events of our lives in our aura as she looked our way, just as she described during the demonstrations when doing readings.

"In the northern hemisphere, the cardinal signs initiate the seasons. When the Sun transits the constellation of Aries, it's springtime, signaling planting season. The sign of Cancer brings in the summer. During autumn, harvest time, the Sun crosses the constellation of Libra. Capricorn begins the winter season. Fixed signs represent the middle period of the seasons. Taurus is when the snow has melted and the ground is thawing in preparation for the budding of plants. The weather starts getting warmer. Leo is the middle of summer and everything is in full bloom. When the Sun is crossing the constellation of Scorpio, the leaves have not yet wilted but are in vivid colors of autumn. Aquarius can be described as being the dead of winter. Mutable signs represent the transitions from the end of one season to the beginning of the next. Gemini is the period ending spring and beginning of the summer. Virgo signals that the heat of summer is cooling as autumn approaches. Sagittarius is the period when preparation for the cold winter is ending. Pisces is the transition of when the Earth starts waking up from its winter slumber and looks forward to spring."

I took copious notes. This description was a revelation to me. The seasonal cycle analogy made sense and helped to memorize which signs were cardinal, fixed, and mutable. Spending most of my life indoors, I forgot that the one-dimensional horoscopic chart plotted with planets wasn't just a theoretical construct on a piece of paper but a practical guide used by farmers who worked outdoors. They needed to be familiar with their environment to ensure the success of their crops. I wondered if the modern-day *Farmers' Almanac* was their astrology handbook.

As I wrote, I continued to observe Iris. She wore a black shirt and pants and gestured with her hands. Her hoarse voice was conversational. There was nothing unusual about her mannerisms. It was her mind that worked differently. She seemed to be aware of my scrutiny because she explained, "When I'm teaching, I have to turn my right brain off since I have to think about what I'm teaching you. I have to be logical." She then continued on with the topic at hand. "Cardinal signs are good at initiating projects." I looked in the direction of her gaze to see if it meant something, to see if the student looked entrepreneurial in some way. I just saw a person who was as intent in writing notes as I was.

As she continued her lecture, I amused myself thinking that her constant peering into the future contributed to her bulging eyes. "Fixed signs persevere to make the project a reality, and the mutable signs are flexible and can adapt to circumstances of endings and changes in plans of a project. Aries can start a project. Taurus works to make Aries's vision a reality. And Gemini will do the marketing."

Iris went back to her seat, pointed to the dry-erase board, and signaled to Étienne, "Draw the natural chart. The natural chart starts with Aries rising. [See the first figure, page 4.] The person's natal chart starts with their rising sign. The Sun or solar sign is based on the day you were born and is aligned with the seasons. The ascendant or rising sign describes which constellation was rising or ascending in the eastern horizon on the hour of birth."

Iris continued, "Sun sign astrology is what you read in the newspapers. It describes a person in general terms." She then asked each of us in which country or state we were born.

I said, "The Philippines." Another said, "Israel." There were people born in Florida, New York, Texas, California, Germany, and India.

Iris said, "Okay, your nationalities are like the sun sign descriptions and generic descriptions of you. Not all Germans are the same. Not all French people or Americans are the same. In the US, people living in different states are not the same. I'm from New York. Once I start talking, you can tell I'm not a Texan. The Sun sign describes you, but it doesn't describe all the details of who you are."

Another analogy she used was that people could be characterized like contents on a product label. We're all basically made of the same stuff with slight variation and proportion of the ingredients. Astrology teaches that the different combinations of five planets and two luminaries plotted in specific locations in an astrological chart can describe traits in human beings.

I had no problem with that reasoning. It reminded me of DNA, which is present in all living things. DNA is encoded with information needed for an organism to develop, survive, and reproduce. It's made of molecules differing only in four building blocks: adenine (A), thymine (T), guanine (G), and cytosine (C). Like the planets and luminaries in astrology, it's the order and placement of the elements that determines DNA's instruction or genetic code. (DNA sequencing is a laboratory technique used to determine the exact sequence of building blocks A, T, G, and C.) Instead of looking down with a high-resolution microscope to view strands of DNA, astrology looks at the night sky above through a telescope at the planetary patterns in the sky and plots them on a horoscope. Iris was describing a sort of astrological DNA, a metaphysical biology.

A few months after I found out about Iris, I booked a reading with her to get more details about my chart and to see how she worked privately. She repeated what she told me during the first demonstration I attended. "You moved a lot, and you will have many more moves."

While she constructed my astrological chart, I looked around her office. The only furniture was her desk and two chairs besides hers. Family pictures were placed in the corner on her right. A large painting of a mountain was on her left. She looked up and followed my gaze. "That's Machu Picchu. A client painted that for me. I was supposed to go with them on a tour. Then, I had a bad feeling about the trip and didn't go. Later, I found out there was an earthquake during that time. I had a feeling." That started her monologue. By now, I knew she was warming up and getting to her heightened state. I followed her instruction that the best way to use her was just to listen and give short answers when asked. And to "write it down."

She stated, "I'm gonna check dates to see if I'm analyzing your chart or if I need to correct the math. What happened when you were six or seven years old?"

I replied, "My family moved from the Philippines to the United States and then, a month after my eighth birthday, I got in a car accident. I stayed in the hospital for three months. My mother said that if I'd died, they would've moved back to the Islands."

"Lucky Jupiter was in your sixth house of health and service," she said. "He helped you and that's why you didn't die. The doctors helped you heal, but you also had luck. The move with your family changed your destiny. Different locations, different people will give different influences, good or bad, depending on the environment and opportunities presented. We're like plants. If someone takes care of us, we can do well. If we're neglected, we won't. An orchid would thrive in Miami but won't do well in the desert unless tended to. But it also depends on your constitution, what your character is. Something happened to you around age twenty-two?"

"That was 1984. I'd just graduated from college. I took a year off before starting medical school." I leaned over the desk to look at her markings on my chart. She pointed to the circled area where 1984 was supposed to be, but I couldn't decipher anything else. I wanted to ask questions about which planetary relationships she was using because how the planets were oriented relative to each other, termed aspects, was how she determined the dates of important events in my life. However, I kept silent because I didn't want to break her train of thought. I'd been to a couple more of her demonstrations to be familiar with her process. I'd come prepared with a list of important dates in my life so that I could give brief answers to confirm what she saw in my chart. I knew that if I kept quiet she would continue to remain in a right-sided frame of mind and I would get more information about my life's movie.

A reading with Iris was more than just an astrological reading. In class she'd say, "The astrologer reads you. The psychic becomes you. I confirm what I see with the astrology."

She made eye contact like we were having a conversation. "What else were you doing?"

I watched her eyes to see if they were focused on me or around me, at my aura. I couldn't tell.

Iris sat behind her desk, alternating her gaze from me to the chart, and pinpointed another important period, asking, "What happened when you were twenty-seven, twenty-eight?"

"I finished med school and moved to New York to continue medical training. I was there for five years."

"I think I got you. The time of birth you gave me was a little off, but I think I rectified your chart. I ask people to give me the time that's written on the birth certificate. Sometimes that's different from what the mother remembers. In some countries, they don't even document the time of birth. Then, I ask questions to see if important events occurred when the chart shows something would've happened. That's how I make sure I'm reading you. By confirming dates in your life, I see if the time of birth that you gave me is correct or if I need to rectify it. Where were you at age thirty-two?"

"I moved to Milwaukee for a fellowship training. I was there for a year. Then I moved to Fort Myers for a job, but that situation didn't work out. I left after six months and found work here."

Having taken some classes with Iris, I had become familiar with the basic outline of my horoscopic chart and the areas of life that the twelve pie-shaped sections represented, such as self, home, career, and family. By sitting with her on a one-to-one private reading, I thought that I would get clues as to how she analyzed the horoscope, but I couldn't follow how her mind worked. I couldn't identify the patterns that directed her questions. Early in the reading, I stopped trying to see where on the chart she was getting information. I would've just shortened my reading by asking her questions and making her shift to the logical left side of her brain. I just listened and took notes. What she had to say about my life was equally as interesting as her process.

I likened Iris's method of explaining a chart to my job as a doctor describing the course of medical disease to my patient. If he or she had a stroke, I might say, "You eat more than enough, and you likely prefer rich food. As you got older, the tendency to develop high cholesterol levels and high blood pressure manifested so that even with exercise and medication, your arteries still built up a lot of cholesterol plaque. You have the genetic predisposition for a cerebrovascular accident (stroke), but it's your environment, having access to rich food, and the habits that you've developed that manifested your stroke."

As a doctor, I studied how a disease progressed and the possible ways it manifested, but I didn't know when organ damage would appear. I didn't know when the heart attack or stroke would happen until the conditions became symptomatic. I only treated the symptoms. Iris had studied what the planets and the different combinations meant from the information passed down from the collective observations of ancient astrologers. She took the birth data of where the planets were located from an ephemeris and then plotted them on an astrological chart. From this map she was able to explain which tendencies would likely manifest in a person's life—and when.

Iris stated, "Astrology is the map of your potential." She'd described the trajectory of my past experiences and how the astrological chart confirmed the choices I made toward higher education. She went on to say, "Your chart is like a road map in time with the starting point being the date, time, and place of your birth. And the planets in the sky don't just stay in one place. As they move in their orbits, I also calculate how the planets evolve in a progressed chart that will also reflect the changes in your life. The planets will move through the twelve different houses in your horoscope and continue to describe how you are changing, how you are maturing in your relationships, work, and even in your home life."

The ephemeris listed dates, times, and locations (in which constellation) where the planets were transiting since my birth. The dates Iris determined to be significant in my life were road signs indicated by specific placement and/or interactions of the planets in the map of my life. The natal horoscope was a map of the planets at the time, day, and location of my birth. The progressed chart mirrored the evolution of those planets over the lifetime of the individual and assisted with the timing of significant events.

Iris taught that astrology can be described as a GPS, a global positioning system, a tool that can provide navigation and timing of a person's life experiences by the position of the planets. But the GPS is dependent on the skill of the map reader, the astrologer. Iris said, "To confirm what I'm seeing for the future, I have to make sure I got your past right."

I thought about the choice my father made to move his family to the United States. If Dad had moved us to Malaysia, his other option instead of America, would my wardrobe consist of headscarves and long skirts instead of jeans and T-shirts? Would I still have become a doctor?

As if reading my mind, Iris explained, "Your Sun and Mercury are strong in the ninth house of higher education. You would've pursued higher education whatever you chose for your career. You're a doctor, but you could've been a professor or gone into religious studies. The ninth house also signifies spirituality and foreign travel. You're gonna travel more. Astrology helps you to become aware of your strengths, weaknesses, and options, so you can make better choices. All the planets contribute to your character. Your Moon and Venus in the tenth house shows that you have a pleasant demeanor, but you also have an aggressive nature with ambitious Mars in its own sign of Aries, living in the eighth house of transformation. You're flexible and can be accommodating, but you're not a pushover. You have Saturn in your fifth house of children, creativity, and intellect. Your Saturn gives you a strong sense of discipline to overcome obstacles, to learn the lessons that he presents to you. It was hard, but didn't you finish medical school? There's a give and take in life; you can't have everything. Saturn also represents limitations and is living in the fifth house, which also represents children. Children are a kind of creativity. It'll be hard for you to have kids. It's not that you can't have children, but there would be obstacles. Are you in a relationship now? Are you interested in pursuing one?"

"No, when I had my accident, I had a lot of internal injuries and surgeries, so I may have adhesions that could complicate a pregnancy."

"How you live your life also depends on your environment. Not just location but who you surround yourself with. You went to my demonstration. You go to astrology classes. You're here now. You're asking questions. This is where you're putting your efforts. Not everybody is supposed to have kids. Not everyone can be a doctor."

The reading with Iris was like an analytic psychotherapy session but using the shortcut of astrology to get to the point in one visit. She homed in on an internal struggle that caused me anxiety but that I had successfully deflected from my consciousness.

My parents realized that through education all their children would achieve a better life than they themselves had. They still held the traditional ideals and wanted their children to get married and have children. I held that ideal also, so much so that when I was eighteen, I had the unrealistic expectation that by the age of twenty-five I would have five children and be in medical school. There was no question in my mind that I would be married as well.

Reality kept getting in the way. After getting established with my career, my attention kept getting sidetracked to more interesting topics, such as how intuitives functioned. During the reading with Iris, I became aware of a part of myself I had not been conscious of. I told myself, it's okay. I had time. My biological clock was not ticking yet. Iris's seemingly innocent comment, "Not everybody is supposed to have kids," hit a chord with me.

Later that afternoon, as I walked on the beach, I thought about what she said. I'd been fooling myself into thinking that I could have it all—a family life, a career, and an unfettered life exploring the esoteric arts. The family life that I laid out as an eighteen-year-old was never going to get off the back burner, but a part of me didn't want to let it go. I still held onto the convictions of my younger self. Unconsciously, I was trying to keep a promise to my eighteen-year-old self whose worldview I had outgrown.

For me, marriage and a family weren't the answer to the question of "What's next?"

Chapter 13:

Que Será, Será.
Whatever Will Be, Will Be

I made it a point to attend Iris's sporadic weekend astrology classes. They were scheduled either Saturday or Sunday. I had weekends off, work was going well, and the class was local, so classes were very convenient. I always arrived early as Étienne was preparing for the workshop. After I helped push chairs into a semicircle, Étienne would list the planetary weather on the dry-erase board. When students showed up, she would ask for their birth data and then hand them back the list of where the planets were located on the day of their birth.

I'd say hello to people as they settled into their seats but quickly returned to reading my notes. While classmates exchanged pleasantries, I reviewed the topics covered in the last session, quietly humming the Doris Day oldie, "Que Será, Será." It became a theme song of sorts whenever I came to class. The song chronicled the advice given to a woman at different stages of her life from childhood to young adulthood. With a carefree heart, she accepted that her future would be determined by fate—whatever will be, will be. When she became a parent and her children inquired about the future, she repeated the advice, describing that the future is a mystery that just unravels. It's not for us to foresee.

The lightness of the tune was a cheerful surrender to fate that never failed to arouse a feeling of longing that the future would be pleasantly taken care of, but now I disagreed with the song's message. My experiences with intuitives over the past several years had shown that the barrier could be penetrated, allowing access to the future through various disciplines. I focused on astrology since it had rules, and the science regarding planetary motion was hard to manipulate.

If I'd been born two hundred years ago, I would have agreed with the lyrics because my choices as a woman would have been limited, especially as a woman of color. Due to the conditions of living off the land, men had a more dominant role. No matter how clever or independent I was, my occupation would've been restricted to cooking, cleaning, and raising children. I would've just been an asset, with my ownership being transferred from father to husband. Maybe I would've been taught the basics of reading and writing, but being a doctor would never have been a consideration.

This kind of deeply rooted cultural belief was part of the Catholic tradition I'd been raised in. The Bible encouraged propagation of the species for survival, with instruction to "Go forth and multiply. Be fruitful and multiply." Leviticus 18:22: "You shall not lie with a male as with a woman; it is an abomination." I questioned my religion since some of the rules didn't make sense. To me, love in its purest form was obviously better than its absence.

I was taught to believe the Bible as truth when attending parochial elementary, middle, and high school. Now, I realized that the biblical elders dictated rules so that their tribes would flourish. Survival of the species was not possible in same-sex relationships, so they used religion to promote their agenda. Large families were also an asset since they provided a built-in workforce. None of this applied to modern-day life.

If propagation of the species was the purpose of the Leviticus verse, then my choice not to bear fruit would also have been considered an abomination. For that matter, heterosexual couples who decided not to reproduce would also be condemned. Some belief systems didn't evolve as the societies that created them transformed. Dogmas were kept even though the original purpose became outdated. I still considered myself a Catholic but one whose worldview had evolved with the educational opportunities of which I took advantage. I believed in some traditions, but others no longer applied to me or to society at large.

It had been a week after my reading with Iris, and I couldn't help thinking that my horoscope reading which had reflected possible obstacles with regard to having children prepared me for discussions on the topic with members of my family. My sister called soon after my appointment and asked, "Don't you want kids? Who's gonna keep you company and care for you when you're older?" I was in my midthirties, she reminded me. "You're getting up there." She even suggested getting information on how to save my eggs—for the future. I made one half-hearted call of inquiry, then dropped it. It wasn't the path I wanted to pursue.

My sister must've spoken to our mother, a devout Catholic, about my biological clock ticking. I tried to pinpoint when the change in Mom had occurred. When I was younger, the rule was marriage first and then have children. Now she was telling me to just have children with no consideration of marriage being discussed. It must've been while she was watching the years progress into my thirties with no hint of a marriage that her point of view relented. Initially, she went along with my dad's insistence to me to "finish school first, then fool around," leading, presumably, to a traditional family situation. Well, I finished school but wasn't hit with the need to marry or have children. Mom called and shocked me. She actually said, "You know, you don't have to marry to have children. If you have kids, I can live with you to take care of them." The wrath of my Catholic God had dissipated.

While pondering this situation, from out of nowhere I snorted, remembering an incident while training as a medical intern in Brooklyn. It was during my internship year in 1990. I was twenty-eight years old and had overnight call duty. A medical student was in the nurses' station. I wasn't in charge of mentoring him, so I didn't greet him. I had work to do, but I did notice that he had a nice physique. If, instead of a white lab coat, he had no shirt and wore leather chamois pants, all the while astride a palomino, he would be the caricature of the Native American Indian epitome we see in old history texts, even with his glasses. I blushed, realizing he reminded me of a college biology professor I'd once had a crush on.

The overhead loudspeaker interrupted my musing as soon as the image came to mind. "GI rounds for internal medicine will start in thirty minutes, fourth-floor conference room." That was how the residents and interns used the hospital PA (public address) system to announce that the pizza we ordered for dinner would be arriving at six o'clock. My focus turned to finishing my charting for the day so that I could catch dinner before it disappeared.

The medical student wanted to have a conversation and called out to me, "Hey, have you ever seen the movie *Angel Heart*, with Lisa Bonet?"

I answered, "No," and continued completing my charts.

He pressed on, "I had a dream last night. There's a scene where she's having sex and then chicken blood starts dripping over her. I looked at her face, and it was you."

"Huh?" If this was a pickup line, I wasn't sure what to make of it. Was he just making conversation? It was weird. I continued my charting and without a moment's hesitation, I dismissed him.

"No, I haven't seen the movie, but when I do, if I do *and* if I have the same dream, I'll let you know, then we'll talk." I was on duty that night, so off I went—alone.

My priority was to get my day's work wrapped up, grab a vacant call room, and get dinner. Resting my head and lying down, even for a few minutes, gave me the opportunity to breathe, calm my nerves, and think clearly for the next twelve hours or more. I had a few hours before the emergency room would page my team to let us know about the patients we would be admitting.

Romantic flirtation was not a high priority for me. Hospital work had girded my loins. Adrenaline was flowing, but in a cerebral direction in anticipation of surviving the night's emergencies. The hot medical student was forgotten. I also had to focus on surviving the evening working with an injured supervising senior resident, Paolo. How was this night going to come off? I'm sure I was paired up with him since I had gained the reputation of being reliable, working efficiently, and doing whatever was needed to facilitate patient care with no attitude. After dinner, I went to meet Paolo to prepare for the night's work.

Paolo was two years ahead of me. He was in his third and last year of the internal medicine residency program and was my assigned resident for the month of September. One weekend last month, he had been drinking and locked himself out of his apartment. He lived in the resident housing complex across from the hospital where we worked. In his inebriated state, he decided to climb the balconies to his second-floor apartment to get inside his home. He didn't make it. The fall left him with two broken legs. What Paolo lacked in insight, he made up with personality. Everyone reacted positively to his easygoing, jovial manner. Anyone else would have been told to take the few months off needed to heal their leg fractures, but he charmed administrators and his fellow residents to accommodate him. So, his injuries meant that I would, literally, be doing all the leg work.

I watched him from the nurses' station, hobbling toward me

on crutches with casts on both legs from mid-thigh to mid-feet. He was comical, greeting the staff on the floor by calling out, "Hey, you got my room ready? I'm your patient tonight." He greeted me in high spirits. "How're you doin?"

I couldn't hide my empathy. "Oh my gosh, why didn't you take a couple of months off?"

"I'm good 'cuz you're gonna be helping me. Nettie's gonna help you too," he said, pointing his head toward the person following him. I smiled and nodded in her direction.

"She's a medical student following me for the day." He then boasted, "My friends are in charge of the ER tonight. They're only going to give us one patient." He then explained how *us* just meant *me*. "Our patient's complicated. She's got a hypercoagulable state and is a high risk for blood clots in her blood vessels, including her brain. She'll need to undergo plasmapheresis or she's gonna stroke out tonight."

"So, what does that mean?" I asked.

"You're going to have to draw one pint of blood from her, go to the blood bank, have them spin the pint, and then transfuse her with the separated red cells. You're gonna have to do it three times to lower her immunoglobulin levels. Page me if you need me." That was code for "I'm going to my apartment across the street to get a good night's rest." My anxiety rose as I watched him turn around, swing his casted legs through crutches, and head toward the elevator, confident that he would get an uninterrupted night's sleep. I was on my own—well, except for Nettie.

What Paolo described was a process similar to dialysis. In dialysis the excess waste products and fluid are filtered externally from the blood, before being transfused back to the person's circulatory system. Tonight, Nettie and I had to do this procedure manually. I started planning. I hoped that my patient had good veins because I needed to get a wide-bore intravenous line started, which had to last for removal of three pints of blood and the subsequent transfusions. Depending on the patient's hydration, it would take thirty to forty-five minutes to withdraw each pint of blood. Then I would have to beg the skeleton staff in the blood bank to do plasmapheresis on the pint of blood, which would take another forty-five minutes, depending on how busy he was. And then, I had to tell him that we had to repeat this sequence three times. The lab tech, begrudgingly, agreed to do what was necessary.

Luck was with me that night. The patient's veins were engorged from the density of the protein in her blood vessels. The wide-diameter plastic IV line easily slid into her vein. I sighed with relief as the rich dark fluid spurted into the plastic bag. Nettie also was a blessing. She ran back and forth to the blood bank located in a connecting building while I coordinated the removal and transfusion of the patient's blood and checked on lab results to monitor that the patient's chemistry was improving.

During medical training, I learned how important it was to get along with everyone—doctors, nurses, radiology techs, housekeepers, etc.—because at more than one point, everyone needs assistance. Patient care was a team effort. During our seven hours of work, Nettie and I guarded our patient from injury. We felt pretty good that our patient slept through most of the ordeal without incident. I'd been too busy to resent Paolo, who got a good night's sleep.

In the ER, Paolo's three friends had been in charge of triaging patients and assigning hospital admissions to all the residents on call. The three buddies hailed from Israel. After finishing their obligation in the army, they attended medical school, then applied and got accepted at this same residency program. They looked out for each other and, apparently, easygoing Paolo. They allowed him to sleep undisturbed and kept their promise not to give his intern, me, more than one patient.

As I signed out my patient to the incoming team, I heard about another third-year resident's experience with the three amigos that night. It made me glad that Paolo, my supervising resident, was well-liked. Mateo was arrogant, rude, and not popular with his peers. So, the three friends were merciless and made him a target. They assigned the more complicated admissions to Mateo's team and he decompensated, overwhelmed with the barrage of sick patients. Mateo took a leave of absence as of that morning.

My astrology class notes from Iris described that Saturn's influence is strong in my chart. Saturn is personified as the teacher who demands discipline from his subjects in order to learn important lessons. Saturn located in my fifth house gives me a strong sense of obligation in the world, but also inhibits the other themes of the fifth house, such as children and romance. My astrological chart opposed the ideals my parents fostered about my having children. It could also be that the influence of Saturn in the fifth house was manifested by the abdominal injuries I sustained in the motor vehicle accident I was involved in when I was eight years old.

My reading with Iris brought to the forefront for me that the goals I had as a young girl were inconsistent with the path I was pursuing as an adult. A part of me longed for my parents' view of happiness: settling down with a husband, children, and a home, with a successful job as a doctor. The childhood goals I had outgrown still had a hold on me. Iris brought my internal conflict into consciousness and let me address the reality that I couldn't have it all and do it all well: the career, the research, and travel with a family. I had to let go of the unconscious guilt of my perceived inadequacies that served no purpose. My strengths were education and curiosity. I needed to channel that energy into tangible pursuits consistent with the trajectory of the path I was forging.

The medical student with his casual remarks meant to divert my interest from work had been easily dismissed without a second thought. My hospital responsibilities were stressful, but they mattered. I berated myself when I couldn't do my best for those I was supposed to help. It buoyed my spirit when a patient got well because of my efforts. My triumphs made my mistakes less difficult to swallow as part of a learning process and pushed me on to the next day.

Responsibility always came first.

"Que Será, Será" came back on auto-repeat in my brain. *So* romantic. *So* hypnotizing. *Whatever will be.* But my thoughts kept interrupting the flow. I didn't believe it anymore. "Whatever will be" didn't just happen. In life, we made choices that, with repetition, became patterns.

Chapter 14:

Meeting a Peruvian Healer in Miami Beach

I continued my lessons with Iris and became more aware that nature's influence on man had become diluted in Western medicine with its emphasis on medical technology. Diagnostic skills were aided by imaging and clinical laboratory data. Manipulation of the laboratory data to normal values dictated treatment to improve the patient's medical conditions.

Western or allopathic medicine had the best tools for acute conditions that needed urgent or emergent attention. If a person was having a heart attack, pain could be alleviated immediately. Cardiovascular surgeons replaced clogged heart vasculature. Ventilator machines inhaled and exhaled for patients with damage to the respiratory centers of the brain. Modern medicine used science. Science gained knowledge through observation of that which could be perceived and measured in the physical, material world, but what could be understood through direct perception was limited. I learned from intuitives who got information from unconventional methods that what wasn't grasped by the senses was both immense and immeasurable.

Edgar Mitchell, the Apollo 14 astronaut and founder of the noetic sciences, said, "There are no unnatural or supernatural phenomenon, only very large gaps in our knowledge of what is natural. We should strive to fill those gaps of ignorance."

Astrology studied the planetary cycles. This was one method of observing our environment as a means to narrow the gap. Science always goes back to the examination of nature. We can't have one without the other. We are part of nature. Man is just one of many different types of animals that can think and manipulate their environment.

I didn't apply the astrological techniques to my patients because it wasn't the standard of care. An astrological consultation was time-consuming since it addressed a person's life history to ensure an accurate chart, not just a medical history. I couldn't ask patients for the location and time of their birth without disclosing my purpose for requesting their information. It wasn't part of the usual patient questionnaire. Patients weren't seeking a reading. I kept the two disciplines separate. My patients expected to be treated with Western medicine, and I practiced Western medicine.

Ancient knowledge of healing captivated me. I wondered more and more how Indigenous healers worked without so much of the hardware used in modern medicine, such as X-rays, magnetic resonance imaging (MRI) scans, and laboratory testing that analyzed blood content. I wanted to learn more about Indigenous medicinal practices. Did men and women called healers, shamans, and medicine men have a different way of knowing about their environment, or did their remedies develop from the method of trial and error? The desire to learn and journey to the places where these medicine people practiced fueled my imagination.

My parents were responsible for our migration to the United States of America. Their stress on education guided me to become a *doktur.* Did their predilection leave an imprint that started the pattern of choices I'd made and had chosen to pursue? Or did my experiences just reflect the ninth house potentials of foreign travel and education present in my chart? I wondered if long-distance travel would manifest as an adult. So far, I'd only been in classroom after classroom. If the potential for distant travel was as strong in my ninth house as my efforts for higher education, then distant travel would materialize. For me, this would strengthen the tenets of the astrology I'd been studying.

One day in early February of 1997, less than a year after relocating to Miami, I saw a sign posted in the mail room of my apartment building. The flyer that caught my eye advertised SAGE, The Society for Advancement of Global Evolution. SAGE had a goal to preserve the wisdom of the Indigenous elders. The organization was sponsoring a Peruvian healer, a *curandero*, who would be lecturing that evening on cross-cultural shamanism, in my building. How convenient was that?

Shamanism is a custom whereby a practitioner participates and/or facilitates a ritual to commune with the spirit world through an altered state of consciousness for a specific purpose. It sounded like a different version of Iris's process, an opportunity I couldn't miss.

There were about fifteen people besides me who showed up in the building's conference room. I didn't recognize anyone. I took a seat in the front by the door so that I could make a quiet exit if the presentation didn't interest me. A projection screen stood at an angle in the corner to the right of where I sat. To the left of the screen, a three-foot-by-three-foot multicolored textile was laid out with many curios similar to souvenirs that one would collect on travels, like rocks and figurines.

Susan, a representative of SAGE, introduced herself and then Oscar. Susan had studied with North, Central, and South

American Indigenous healers and wisdom keepers, including Oscar, the Peruvian *curandero*. He had trained in ethnopsychology in the United States and described his practice as a fusion of both ancestral Andean traditions along with "heart-sourced spiritual paths."

Oscar looked to be in his late thirties or early forties. He was stocky with wavy dark-brown hair and piercing eyes. His mischievous smile welcomed the attendees. He pointed to the woven blanket on the floor and explained that this manta and the sacred objects on top made up his Pachakuti mesa. It represented his practice, a combination of southeastern Andean mystical and northern, coastal Kamasqa *curanderismo* traditions. My understanding of a shaman was a person in a tribal community who acted as an intermediary between the seen and unseen worlds for a specific purpose, usually curing ailments. Oscar made it a point to explain that he considered shamans to be aboriginal, those without contact with the modern world. He was a healer but not a shaman. It seemed like an opinion that showed reverence for the purity of the ancestral tradition.

After introducing himself, he told us we would be participating in a ritual that would explain how he used the mesa. The lights dimmed and he positioned himself behind his display of objects, facing the attendees. Oscar wore an earthen-colored poncho with a similar weaving to the manta. He picked up a conch shell, faced the ceiling, and began blowing on the instrument with all his might. It brought to mind the vision of angels blowing trumpets to herald a great event. Then, he started an invocation in English and another language I didn't recognize. The scene had the effect of transporting the group to the wilderness of the Andean mountains with a local healer.

I wondered if any of the people in the lobby would come in to see what the ruckus was about. No one came.

Oscar lit a sage bundle and, with a two-foot-long feather in his other hand, he crouched as he waved the smoke to the four directions of his mesa. He began explaining the position and placements of the objects on the manta. His voice thundered, "I call upon the five directions to join our group tonight. Pachamama, representing Mother Earth, is located in the southern direction; Mama Killa, the Moon, in the west; Viracocha, the Supreme Creator, in the north; and Inti, the Sun, is in the eastern direction. The fifth direction is in the center. It is here that the rainbow spirit resides in the realm of wholeness and transformation. Its element is quintessence." The *curandero* was in a deep reverie.

From where I sat in the audience, I thought we would just be observing the ceremony, but then Oscar started walking around the room surrounding all of us attendees in a circle of sage smoke, explaining that smoke cleared our space from unwanted spirits. As he moved, he kept an even, hypnotic pace to his words. "The five directions are associated with specific animal guides. These spirit creatures guide and protect anyone who identifies with them on his or her life's journey."

He expanded on the story of each direction: the candle in the east, the place of the Sun, Inti, symbolized fire, representing the mind. Its tutelary animals were puma and jaguar. The south was Mother Earth, the physical, symbolized by a stone and associated with the boa or anaconda. A shell for the Moon in the west represented flowing water, the emotional realm with the spirit animals of dolphin and whale. In the north, a feather for Viracocha, the Supreme Creator, represented spirituality, the element of air connected with the condor and eagle.

When he returned to the front of the room, Oscar knelt behind the mesa, facing us. He waved the sage smoke with his feather over the center, where a large cross was placed. With a reverent tone, he explained, "The center, K'uychi, the rainbow bridge, grounds the energy of mesa. Your most sacred objects are placed here." He described that the rainbow bridge connected all the directions. Its spirit animals are the llama and alpaca, symbolizing strength and endurance.

Oscar laid down the sage bundle on an abalone shell and picked up a slender fluid-filled bottle. He took a mouthful of the perfumed water, not swallowing it but spraying it over the objects on the mesa. He then walked over to Susan and with another mouthful of liquid sprayed the front and backside of her body, including her face. *From his mouth!* I watched as she lifted her arms so that Oscar could brush the air beneath and over her arms with his feather. He continued along the perimeter of her body. He later explained that he was "cleaning her aura."

I hoped this part of the ritual wouldn't entail audience participation, or that he would ask permission first, but he went straight to the person closest to him in the front row and completed the same ritual of cleansing. I thought of saying no thank you, but decided to go along with the aura purification since I didn't have far to travel until I could take a shower.

Oscar went around to each person in the room, taking small mouthfuls of Florida water prior to spraying us with the cleansing liquid from his mouth. Then, he brushed our auras with his feather. This ritual with the sage and the Florida water was supposed to remove negative energy and make us receptive to connection with the unseen entities.

Afterward, Oscar went back to his mesa to call in our ancestors and all the creatures of nature to commune with the group for our highest good. He continued his invocation, replacing the feather in his hand with a rattle and shaking it over the sacred objects on the manta. The *curandero* emphasized in a slow, intentional manner, "Placement of the mesa in the same way over and over gains power through repetition. These medicine pieces in the Pachakuti tradition have an energy of their own. They carry a wisdom of their own, and it is through the wisdom of these artifacts that the Pachakuti practitioner is able to work the planetary forces for benevolent social change. Your items that you place will be personal to you. Each person's mesa will look different because it will be a reflection of the mesa carrier." He explained that the tools chosen from the five directions were used to restore wholeness from ailments that had symbolic etiology from the elements of earth, water, air, and fire.

I didn't know if any of the other audience members had ever experienced such a ceremony before, but it reminded me of mass in my Catholic tradition, only more dramatic in some aspects. I likened Oscar to a robed priest who preached in Latin as he raised his hands and countenance to the heavens, transforming the bread and wine into the body and blood of Christ. Both the *curandero* and priest were animated as they converted the ordinary items to articles of power.

During special celebrations like Easter and Christmas, the priest used liturgical implements to bless the congregation and repel evil. An aspergillum, a metal wand that held liquid, was used to sprinkle holy water, and a censer, an incense burner attached to a chain, would be waved around the congregation. The *curandero* waved a sage wand and used himself as the vessel to sprinkle cleansing water.

Oscar closed with a meditation on the Incan prophecy, "We are coming to an age when the eagle of the north and the condor of the south fly together." He explained that North and South America were starting to work together, unite, as evidenced by bringing his South American traditions to North America. "We depend on Mother Earth, Pachamama. We are all native, because the word *native* comes from nature. We are all parts of Mother Nature. We need to take care of each other."

There was a slideshow afterward showing the landscape and people of the Peruvian Andes. He talked about conducting ceremony and pilgrimage to sacred sites, including Machu Picchu, the symbol of the Incan empire. He was planning an upcoming South American trip so that participants could experience healing energy work in Peru.

The evening demonstrated some aspects of *curanderismo* healing. Oscar showed how he used ritual and intention to activate the tools on his mesa, similar to an altar, for his sacred objects. I saw how he called on the unseen entities to aid in his medicine work. The ritual and the unfamiliar language allowed a glimpse into an intangible world that was reality for a remote, contemporary culture that utilized ancient wisdom. I was aware of energy work, which seemed to be what Oscar used in his medicine practice. I understood that shamanic healing is not based so much on treating specific pathogens but on restoring balance between the elements of nature present in the person. We were part of nature.

I believed in ritual. I grew up not to question that my priest transformed the bread and wine into the body and blood of Christ, and that's why I took Holy Communion even when I didn't go to confession or mass regularly. It led to salvation. With religion, I had faith. I didn't need to prove anything to anybody. I didn't have to answer to anyone but myself. But the healing tradition I learned was scrutinized by peers and relied heavily on physical results. Allopathic medicine puts emphasis on treating illness by measuring data and administering medication that changes chemistry. I believed in the unseen energy because I saw the effects of X-rays and CT scans, which used invisible energy to create images. Radiation therapy kills cancer cells. The Sun's energy, ultraviolet rays, cause sunburn. A microwave oven heated my coffee.

In allopathic medicine, we strived to work in a sterile environment. Oscar used sacred smoke and perfumed water sprayed from his mouth. He called on the spirits of the five directions. It ignited my imagination. I wasn't caught between the two worlds of healing; I could believe in both and just be proficient in one. The doctor in me realized that there were limitations in my field of medicine, and I was curious about this process because using unseen energies to heal was a concept foreign to how I worked in Western medicine. I didn't know how to measure it. I needed to learn more about it.

I also wondered whether the shamanic tradition, integrating nature with healing, could be packaged and sold to modern medicine. I doubted that pharmaceutical companies would promote the work if they couldn't secure economic rights to consciousness and spirit allies.

The modern medicine I learned did not think about consciousness, the full activity of the mind and senses. It did not think about the healing power of spirit, because anything that couldn't be measured or observed was not considered in the healing process. If this man could call on unseen nature to effect healing at will, he had a fantastic skill.

Self-analysis of my astrological chart became a constant practice. It helped me understand my life situations by seeing how the astrological teachings were embodied in my life and how I behaved. I was born with the constellation of Virgo rising, which is an earth sign ruled by Mercury. The description "down-to-earth" suggests practicality and sensibility. In my case, the drive toward gathering knowledge from the five senses originated from Taurus ruling my ninth house of higher education. If Mercury was placed in a house owned by Scorpio, the most sexual sign of the zodiac, the data I would be gathering from the five senses would be sexually oriented.

The sign of Virgo is known as the critic of the zodiac because it has a great ability to discriminate. Virgo's symbol is the maiden separating the wheat from the chaff, distinguishing what's useful from that which is not digestible by humans.

Mercury, known in mythology as the winged messenger, also rules the constellation of Gemini, an air sign, and represents thoughts and communication. Geminis are curious and have the ability to make connections and talk with everyone. However, the Virgo part of me discriminates with whom I wish to make connections. Gemini owns my tenth house and describes the knowledge base behind my career. Its symbol is the twins, similar but separate. I began to better understand my dual nature in the layers of astrological tenets. I worked in Western medicine but was still curious about other methods of diagnosis and healing. My Gemini side wants to gather information from different sources. The Virgo side of me analyzes all the collected data to see what is practical and useful. The Taurus in me, which owns the ninth house of higher learning and long-distance travel, is the most sensual sign of the zodiac. Its sensuality wants the experience for the senses, of interacting with different people who practice the esoteric arts. Taurus wants to travel to the places where various types of healing methods are practiced and not just read about them.

After the demonstration, I introduced myself to Susan since she wasn't surrounded by as many people as Oscar. I thanked her for the evening's event. I told her I was a physician and that I was interested in learning more about shamanism.

She said SAGE was based in my building and she lived here as well. "Write down my number," she said. "Let's talk some more. We're having a trip to Peru in a couple months. Think about going."

The next couple of nights, I had a recurring dream of myself as a man walking through wilderness, mountains, valleys, and along cliffs, just walking. It was a vivid, recurring dream that I'd had when I was in my early twenties but had forgotten about. It meant nothing to me then. The man in the dream was tall with brown hair and dark skin. He was mature. He looked to be in his midthirties, my age now.

In this dream, I observed this man, who I sensed was me, and wondered where he was going. I felt him to be in search of something. During the day, he walked continuously with the goal to just move forward. The only time he stopped was at night after the Sun went down. Before he slept, he would gaze for a long time at the lights in the sky and wonder what was out there.

The dream seemed like a faded memory of a familiar path that was renewing itself in my consciousness. The circumstances of the journey had faded, but the man's feeling of wonder, curiosity, and purpose stayed with me. It was the same feeling I got when I walked for hours through the streets of New York City, the same feeling I got now when I'd walk the length of Miami Beach. My breath deepened.

One morning after waking up from this dream, I decided to construct a mesa, following Oscar's instructions. I was used to ritual. I went to church weekly growing up. Nightly, my mother lit a candle on her bedroom dresser from dusk until she went to sleep. Two pictures stood by the candle. One was of Jesus Christ with his burning heart encircled by thorns with fire rising to a cross. The heart signified Christ's divine light of love for mankind. The other was a serene portrait of the Virgin and Child. Mom would recite her rosary as she lay down to sleep. Sometimes I would peek in and mischievously ask, "Are you praying for me?" She would open her eyes, look at me, and say, "Always, *anak ko* [my child]," and then go back to her rosary.

When I was a child, her devotion to the routine made an impression on me because she was praying outside of church. Over the years, I adopted the practice of lighting candles to recreate the stillness I felt from her habit; sometimes it would be for a spiritual purpose, but mostly, just for quietness.

In Miami there were many Latinos who practiced Christianity. Use of candles was common, and the grocery stores routinely carried inexpensive prayer candles called *veladoras*. They were eight-and-a-half-inch circular glass containers with colorful images of different saints on one side and a prayer on the other. I usually picked the ones with the likeness of Jesus Christ or the Virgin Mary. If I found one with a portrait of Saint Anthony of Padua, I got that as well. He was the patron saint of lost or stolen items to whom I'd prayed many times to help me find myself.

I believed in Oscar's ritual, and shamanism seemed to be the direction that my path was leading me. As I further explored my interest in the divination arts, my goal went from questioning the practitioners about my future to seeking ways to learn their skills. The ceremony that Oscar demonstrated provided another opportunity to learn.

I felt hesitation with carrying out the mesa rite. As a child of five or six, I felt the presence of beings that I didn't understand. I would wake up at night and look around knowing somebody was there. I never thought to tell my parents, since in church I was used to praying to people I couldn't see. Instead, I decided to take matters into my own hands and made a deal with the beings. Before I went to sleep, I told them, "I don't want you to come to me during the day because you're gonna scare me if I see you, but you can come and talk to me in my dreams when I'm sleeping." They honored my request. But now I felt anxious because I worried that opening myself up to shamanism might encourage encounters with the entities I'd asked not to see as a child.

Curiosity won out. On a white handkerchief used as a manta, I honored the Pachakuti tradition and positioned items on the coffee table I'd collected as souvenirs: an onyx rock in the southern direction, a shell in the west, a feather in the north, and a votive in the east. For the center rainbow bridge, I placed a *veladora* with an ornate image of Christ. After closing the shades, I sat on the floor across from the windows, facing north, and started. I lit the candles and set an intention to carry out the ritual with reverence.

Oscar said that the Pachakuti mesa evolved over the years. During the Spanish conquest, the practitioners incorporated Christianity into their ceremonies so that their traditions would survive, which explained the cross in the center of his mesa. I didn't understand the foreign language that Oscar used, so I decided my invocation would begin with prayers that I knew, the Lord's Prayer, a Hail Mary, and a prayer to my guardian angel. With trepidation, I then mimicked Oscar and called in my ancestors and the spirits of the plant and animal kingdom. All at once, I heard a zipping noise as the shade in front of me rolled up to the ceiling, slamming open. At the same time, the glass on the candle cracked on the image of Jesus Christ. Whoa!

I broke out in a cold sweat. What spirit did I call in? The exploration of this mystery was not under my control. I didn't know what to do. After my shock, I dismantled the mesa and quickly left to go to work.

When I got home, I called Susan and told her what happened. She came down to my apartment to look around. I told her, "The ceremony looked simple. The mesa was easy to set up. I thought I would just be praying and meditating. All of a sudden, the shade zipped up and the candle cracked. Scared me."

The first thing she told me was, "You didn't clear out the unwanted spirits."

"What do you mean?"

"Did you use sage?"

"No."

She asked me to show her where I'd sat and which shade had opened. She carried a woven backpack made of the same brown textile as Oscar's poncho. "This is my medicine bag," she said. On the coffee table, she laid out some of the contents. She showed me her eagle feather used as a wand. "Oscar's is a condor feather," she commented.

"Ahh, the Incan prophecy. The eagle of the North and the condor of South America working together. I get it."

"This is Florida water," she said, handing me the slender bottle.

The ornate label read: *Florida Water, Cologne*. I looked at her curiously and asked, "Perfume is what you guys use to cleanse the aura?"

"Yes, this one has high vibrational energy." She opened it and poured some in my hand and told me to "wash" it over my body.

Then, she passed the feather around by body, "to smooth out your aura." As she moved her feather, I told her in disbelief, "I can feel it, wherever you wave the feather, I feel an electricity-like tingle." I kept watching and it was just a feather, not attached to any outlet. I was awestruck.

"That's energy work, sister."

She then walked around my apartment and stopped at different spots. When she got to the windows that looked out onto my balcony, she turned to me and pointed to the caramel-colored velour armchair positioned under the shade that had flown open and asked, "Where did you get this?"

"At a flea market in Fort Myers. It was in great condition. I got a deal for twenty-five bucks."

"Well, it's been reupholstered. It belonged to a crochety old woman. And she wanted you to know you disturbed her. She won't stop complaining."

I followed as she walked toward the balcony door, behind my panel screen room divider that sectioned the alcove where I had a sofa bed for visiting friends. My eyes just got wider as she told me more. "You know, there are a lot of older people that move to Florida. There was a man who was very sick and died here. He hasn't moved on to the light."

I wasn't surprised by the revelation. "When my friends sleep here, they all tell me that they don't sleep well," I told her. "But when my dad slept here, he had no problems. But I'll tell you, the spirit of the person who passed here was probably more scared of my dad, because he can be a son of a gun to deal with. Well, what can I do?"

"Before I managed SAGE, I cleaned houses—not housekeeping, though. I cleared spirits from haunted homes. I had a good business but gave it up to do medicine work. Gunther, who's funding SAGE, plans on setting up a healing spa in this complex, next to the gym, for energy work."

Susan continued, "I can help you. I can't tell ya how important it is that before you do any ritual, you need to clean your space of unwanted spirits. If you don't, you open yourself up to negative energy when you call in all the spirits. You woke up the two living here. One pulled up your shade, and the other broke the glass on your candle."

She opened my balcony door, then lit her sage bundle and walked around the apartment, into all the rooms, including the closets and the bathrooms, waving the sage fumes with her feather into every corner of the apartment, saying, "Only love and light reside here." In the alcove, she spoke to the entity and said a prayer. The last thing I heard was, "Follow the light," as she waved it through the open balcony door. When she got to my armchair, she first waved sage smoke all over it. "This woman is nasty," she commented. Susan then said some more prayers and beckoned to the woman, "You have to go to the light now," sweeping the eagle feather toward the open balcony door to show her the way. "C'mon, it's time," she coaxed.

Then, she turned to me and repeated, "You always have to protect your space when you're doing energy work. That's the first thing I learned when doing medicine work. Protect yourself first, then you can work on someone else."

"How did you start working with Oscar?" I'd always been interested in how people started working in these offbeat occupations. Did she start out as a housekeeper and then find she had a knack for clearing spirits from homes? This was a good way to lead to more questions about how she could communicate with spirits.

"Well, you wouldn't think it, with my blond hair and blue eyes, but I'm part Native American with a Southern Baptist background. I grew up in the shadow of Stone Mountain, Georgia. My grandmother was Cherokee, and she taught me about the sacred connection of all life. As I got older, I started having experiences with the spirit world, and I tried to get away from it by getting into all sorts of things. I had a choice to face what I was and work with it, or end up in an institution. That's when I started honoring my healing heritage."

I liked Susan right away. I felt more at ease since she cleared my home. She was so comfortable with this medicine work and dealing with the unseen. I felt this woman had a genuine gift. The electricity I felt when she passed her eagle feather around my body was real. I was excited to meet another person who could communicate with unseen entities. And she seemed open to sharing her experience and knowledge. I told her of my interest and journey in the esoteric arts. "When I saw the flyer about SAGE in the mail room, I knew I was being presented with another opportunity to experience."

"I met Oscar through a client," Susan told me. "I asked to apprentice with him because I connected with his powerful message. I've been to Peru and met with the other *curanderos,* and I felt such pure energy there." She looked at her watch and said, "Hey, I gotta go, but I want you to think about going to Peru. You need to experience it. Our message will have more impact if a Western doctor can describe it."

I thanked her and promised to seriously think about it.

After that evening, I kept a mesa with my sacred objects on a side table but I never called on spirits like I did that first time. I would just light a candle, say my prayers, or just be quiet.

I had become my mother.

Chapter 15:

If It Is Your Adventure, the World Will Open for You

About two weeks after my house was cleansed from unwanted spirits, I spoke to Iris about the Peru trip. "For me, I don't need to be in an airplane to fly. I travel all the time," she said. "My brain takes me to many different places. But you, that's how you learn. The tendencies show in your ninth house, signifying education and long-distance travel. You don't have to go, but you will have opportunities. It's just like if a person has a good chart for romance but then decides to stay home all the time. No relationship will manifest if that person doesn't make the effort. The stars impel, they don't compel."

Then she spoke about timing. "You couldn't have traveled to foreign countries before. You had to prepare. You needed to learn to be a doctor so you can have a perspective about different healing techniques. Plus, you needed to be able to make a living so you can afford to travel. You can't just show up and expect people to take care of you. You're in a good position now."

In a taped lecture, Joseph Campbell, a professor of literature who worked in comparative mythology and applied the stories to the human condition, said, "There are two kinds of adventures. One is the one that is yours. It has come to you in a way of inner voice or readiness for a certain kind of adventure. The other is following a crowd."

I had followed the crowd, initially, going through traditional schooling. Campbell described accurately what I felt: "Then you come to the edge of the world, that place, psychologically, that no one has explored for you, that you have to do on your own; before that you are in, more or less, mapped-out territory."

Many of the Native American mythologies described a Spider Woman. She represented wisdom and education. She appeared as a teacher, guide, and protector. In the Navajo tradition, she taught the art of weaving textiles to use and sell for winter survival. In the Hopi tradition, Spider Woman guided creature travelers to higher worlds, mentoring them as they changed into different forms and slowly became human.

Iris personified a type of Spider Woman for me. She taught me to spin threads, the rules of astrology, in the horoscopic wheel. This knowledge helped me gain insight into the web of my life. It taught me about the patterns of my past and how I could weave texture into my future.

I resonated with Campbell's statements about adventure. "If it is yours, the world will open. Where other people will run into obstacles, blocks, it will open for you. You get on the road and thumbing your way, a car that stops has the people in it that are just the ones that can carry you that distance, give you advice or perhaps a five-dollar bill that can carry you the rest of the way. All that kind of thing—magical aid."

Susan and Oscar were the people in that car that stopped by to carry me part of the way.

Two months later, I found myself in a South American jungle, on a two-and-a-half-hour motorized launch on the Tambopata River, a tributary of the Amazon, headed to a lodge north of the Reserva Nacional Tambopata in the southeastern region of Madre de Dios. Twenty-two of us from different parts of the United States met in Lima. After our one-night stay in the Peruvian capital, we set out early to catch a flight to Puerto Maldonado. Upon landing, we rode a bus to the river port.

The Amazon River had no directional markers that I could identify. The guides seemed to depend on the landscape for orientation. The indentations of the shoreline, along with different types of vegetation, took the place of road markers. I could've been on the Mississippi River since all I saw was dense greenery on either side of the shore. I watched the scene as it melded with the animated mental picture of where I was on the globe, gliding along on the world's longest river in the famed Amazon jungle with a feeling of incredulity. Indeed, I was no longer in a classroom.

The Sun was not quite overhead, but it was already hot and humid. There was a bird or two that flew overhead against the canopy of blue sky, but no other animals were in sight; likely they were sheltering from the heat.

The only noise that I could hear was from the motorized canoe we had settled in. The sunlight gave the water a murky, bluish-green color, but closer to the boat it was clear. The launch had a roof but was otherwise uncovered and allowed an unfettered view of the scenery. Each person sat on either side of the boat separated by a narrow aisle. I reached my hand out to skim the river water as the canoe propelled forward but quickly retracted my arm remembering that caimans, related to the alligator, inhabited these parts.

Western medicines came from these huge forests. The "flying death" was one way of describing poison-tipped arrows used by skilled hunters to take down prey or enemies. The active compound was curare, a substance obtained from the bark and stems of a South American plant and also utilized in the field of anesthesia to temporarily paralyze muscles during surgery. Quinine for treatment of malaria came from the cinchona tree of South America. And spices such as vanilla, ginger, and cinnamon originated in the rain forests.

On the way to our jungle lodging, the loud whirring of the boat's motor allowed only for conversation with the person next to you. It didn't matter because we all were taking in the view, excited for our adventure.

The motor quieted as the canoe slowed down, giving Oscar the opportunity to set the backdrop for the night's ayahuasca healing ceremony. "We're going to make a stop and pick up the Don Ignacio." Don and Doña were the customary titles of respect for people of importance in local communities. He explained, "*Curanderos* are self-reliant. They prepare their medicine, picking the shrubs, herbs, and grasses from their surroundings. Ayahuasca is made from two sacred plants. Don Ignacio takes several days to produce this liquid. He prays to the spirit of the plants to help him choose which ones are ready to help the people partaking of the ritual. The plants sing to him when they are ready. With the aid of the healer, this spiritual medicine can safely open the portals of the mind to another dimension."

Ayahuasca is a sacred brew containing the hallucinogenic drug dimethyltryptamine (DMT), used for ritual, medicinal, and recreational purposes. (What's interesting is that one of the plants containing DMT belongs to the genus *Psychotria*, in the coffee family of Rubiaceae. Coffee is not considered a harmful drug in the modern culture, but it does have psychoactive effects of increasing mental alertness, and in excess, it can cause jittery sensations, high blood pressure, increased heart rate, and sweating.) When ingested alone, the gut enzymes can degrade the DMT, rendering the substance inactive.

Liana, a woody vine, is the other ingredient in the mix. It deactivates the gut enzyme, allowing the psychoactive properties of DMT to function. I was hesitant to take spiritual medicine that could alter my perceptions in the rain forest, far from my familiar hospital environment. What if I had a bad reaction and needed Western medical services? I also disliked ingesting slurries of any kind, and Oscar's description that Don Ignacio spit in the mixture to activate the preparation didn't appeal to my background of using sterile medication.

The engine puttered as we slowly approached the location where the *curandero* would join us. A small, thin man dressed in well-worn pants, short-sleeved shirt, and hat made his way through the brush to get down to the river's edge. Oscar met him, took a jug from him, and helped him onto the boat. The jug, I assumed, contained the ayahuasca. I snapped a picture of what looked like a rat lagging behind the medicine man. It was the size of a small dog. I hoped that thing wasn't going to join us.

We arrived at the Tambopata Lodge in the early afternoon, allowing for time to have a light lunch, rest, and then explore or take a swim. A clearing in the jungle housed separate accommodations for men and women. There were separate open-air huts for the kitchen and dining areas, as well as an enclosed meeting place. The wooden framework made the construction of the straw huts sturdy enough to support proper doors and windows with straw shutters. There was even a shower and toilet for the five people who shared my hut. I didn't want to think about where the sewage drained.

We were given instructions as to where the safe waters were located for swimming. Before dinner, the more adventurous among us went to swim in a watering hole that a guide described as inaccessible to caimans. The lodge was located at the northern boundary of the Reserva Nacional Tambopata, which had over one thousand square miles of preserved land with many diverse habitats.

A group of us walked to the area where we could swim. There was forest and then water with no intervening shore to speak of. I don't swim but waded for a few minutes close to the rocky ledge that we walked down. I wanted bragging rights to say that I swam in the cool waters of an Amazon River basin.

Curious about the energy of the rain forest and more sure-footed on land, I left my companions to wander along the safety zone of the settlement, looking for macaws and monkeys and avoiding the scorpions. As the Sun went down, the jungle woke up with the rhythmic sound of insects and chirping birds. The stars started becoming visible with so little light pollution to obscure them. And then, it was time to meet for dinner.

The ayahuasca ceremony was scheduled after dinner. We were told not to overeat as the preparation had a purging effect, but I couldn't help myself. The delicious meal consisted of fresh fish, fruits, and vegetables. Don Oscar waited until after dinner to tell us about Don Ignacio's vision. The healer foresaw that one of us would become blind during the ritual. Don Oscar expressed his concern that this event would indeed occur. He asked if we wanted to proceed.

We, as a group, were excited to be in the Amazon and weren't fully convinced of the gravity of the elder's warning. Overcome with anticipation for a mystical experience, we all agreed to proceed. I wondered if I would be the one to go blind, but I didn't want to miss the opportunity to see what this ceremony was all about. Two in our group decided to participate in the ceremony but not partake of the ayahuasca. Oscar gave us the option to change our minds. I opted to see how the evening went in deciding whether I would drink the brew or not.

We met in a hut on stilts. After choosing what would be our seats on the floor for the next couple of hours, the lights were turned off and Don Ignacio started the ceremony. Oscar had already cleansed us with Florida water. The torches marking walkways outside outlined Don Ignacio's shadow as he sat in front of the open window. He prayed to the spirits of the plant medicine to grace our journey. Amid the darkness, the *curandero* chanted *icaros*, magical prayers for healing, then passed the slurry around. Each person had the choice to take a swig or a sip. Rhythmic rustling of his *chacapa*, a rattle made from a bunch of palm fronds tied together, accompanied his muted hypnotic tones, *Ma Ri Ri Ri Ri Ri Ri Ri Ri Ri Ri Ri Ri Ri Ri Ma Ri Ri Ri*. The songs were directed to the nonphysical guides of the psychoactive vegetation. They would decide whether the individual's experience would be joyful or traumatic.

I only took a taste of the thick bitter liquid, not even a sip, but its effects surprised me. After a few minutes, as the rhythm and tone of the *curandero's* chant varied, I felt the rise and fall of the figurative Kundalini serpent in my belly. With so many participants, the temperature in the room was rising. My sweating from the heat and humidity was compounded with the nausea that washed over me.

In Sanskrit, *Kundalini* means a "coiled snake." It is an energy center located at the base of the spine. Once activated, the serpent rises and can awaken the energy centers located higher and parallel to the spine. The reptile wanted to be released from its physical prison. I felt the slow ascension of the snake making its way up the path toward each chakra, persistent against my efforts to tamp it down.

As the liquid seeped into our consciousness, the purging began. The physical action of the brew was to cleanse the body, either by vomiting or diarrhea. As the room got warmer, I heard people around me begin to shift positions on the floor, then I heard quickened steps to the doorway, followed by heaving and retching. This initiation preceded the mind-expanding experience—if physical discomfort didn't hinder the process; some people left to go back to their huts because of the overwhelming cleansing effects.

I hated to vomit. I kept telling myself that it was just a bad reaction to the ayahuasca. *Just breathe in and out, and your stomach will settle down.* I kept tamping down the serpent. *You can control this,* I repeated to myself. I looked around and saw the shadows of the Georgia couple slumping down to the right of me, blocking the little bit of cool breeze coming from the opened doorway. Sweat dripped from my forehead. As they stretched on the floor, the sour smell from their vomitus wafted my way. Adding to my queasiness, the stench lingered and combined with the perfumed Florida water and sage smoke that Oscar had used to purify each of us prior to the ceremony. With the humidity, the odors hovered around me and kept breaking my concentration in my battle to keep the serpent from rising.

"Help me! I can't see."

It was a woman's voice. It was too dark to see who had cried out. Hushed voices communicated in the corner of the hut. The ceremony continued for those already in reverie. Oscar and Don Ignacio continued to monitor the effects of the medicine on the remaining participants, all the while attending to the woman who'd become blind.

One by one, each of us retreated to our huts. I wanted to see the ceremony through to the end, but after four hours, I realized the *curanderos* were going to stay as long as there were participants having their experiences. Discussion about the effects bestowed by the plant spirit of the medicine would have to wait until morning.

Walking back to my hut, I met up with a couple of my roommates. They were looking at the night sky. I looked in the direction of their gaze. One of them told me, "It's a spaceship."

The four of us kept looking at the oval shape in the sky and tried to rationalize what it was. I told them, "It can't be a cloud since it's got a perfect oval shape. It's solid, because I can't see the stars through it."

Other people who were not in our group were looking in the same direction. I heard one say, "I think the star brothers are watching us." They didn't use the term "aliens." This was in keeping with Oscar's teaching on Peruvian cosmology. The sky and star systems were a continuation of nature on Earth, and the inhabitants of the cosmos were distant relatives.

No one got abducted that night, but I kept thinking how unusual it was for a group of people to have the same hallucination. After minutes of staring at the night sky, we all decided it was time to lie down and get some sleep.

The serpent in my belly continued to rise even without the snake charmer's hypnotic chant. Breathing the cool night air helped to force it down. I thought that my struggle with the serpent was won, but then I had to turn back to the ceremonial room. I had left our hut key on the floor beside me.

Upon reentering the space, I felt as if I'd passed through an invisible barrier. The *curanderos* were still there and the energy in the hut lingered like clear fog. I was caught off guard and the serpent gained enough strength to release itself from its physical confinement. I turned around and retched just outside the door. I stood hypnotized, gazing at the white aura surrounding my vomitus.

It was Donatella who'd gone blind. We were sitting together at breakfast when she told me. With the past evening's nausea gone, my appetite was stronger than ever.

Donatella worked with Oscar's group, his ayllu, on the West Coast. At forty years old, five years older than me, she exuded a happy-go-lucky, loud, overly friendly personality—especially toward men. She flirted with all the males in the group, including the guides, who misinterpreted her flirtation as genuine interest. Men attended to her, and to me when I accompanied her. It made me uncomfortable. Early on, I told her, "It's not good to flirt with the locals. They don't know you're just playing. One day, you're going to take it too far." She laughed at me, saying, "Loosen up. Have fun. It's only three weeks."

Donatella told me, "The ayahuasca took me back to when I was getting counseling about three years ago." She relived a dark episode as she described what happened.

"You are very relaxed. You will remember nothing when you wake up," her psychotherapist told her many times as he put her under hypnosis.

In their last session, Donatella found herself above her physical body, looking down at herself. "I couldn't believe what I was seeing. My therapist was raping me, and I couldn't move. He was supposed to be helping me!"

Her breathing mimicked what she described to me. "I watched as my breathing became faster and faster until it stopped. Last night, it was so real. I didn't want to see it. All I knew when I opened my eyes was darkness, no light. I calmed down after Oscar said, 'Sister, it's over. You survived the violation.' When my vision returned, I saw Oscar and Ignacio's faces and they knew, they knew what happened. I didn't have to tell them. I thought I was over it."

The next day was our last and more idyllic, sightseeing around the encampment, swimming, and an evening ceremony with the *curanderos* but no further use of the psychoactive brew. I wandered, looking at my surroundings with wonder. There are eighty thousand species of plant life in the Amazon rain forest, including the trees, shrubs, bushes, and vines. There are over twenty-five hundred species of lianas. How did the Indigenous people distinguish the two plants that contained chemicals that when combined could cause a mind-altering experience that would enable them to access wisdom? And without the technology with which modern civilization prides itself?

Without instruments to analyze chemicals, the only method of analysis that made sense was trial and error. Or did the plants really sing to the healers? To survive, Indigenous people had to know their environment intimately. They revered nature as alive with the ability to communicate. They utilized a different type of knowing. They took care of the rain forest that took care of them.

As we left the Tambopata Lodge, our canoes skimmed along the sunlit Amazon River. I smiled, taking in the lush green rain forest on either side. I envisioned a mental cartoon image of our canoe on a globe as a pin moving through a branch of this famed waterway back to Puerto Maldonado.

We were on a pilgrimage and conducting rituals in the sites sacred to the ancient people of Peru who honored the healing power of their environment. By bringing foreigners to learn the traditions of their past, Oscar hoped to reignite interest in his own people. By seeing the reverence with which outsiders viewed their rituals, Oscar hoped to encourage Peruvians to value and preserve their heritage.

Oscar spoke about three worlds in the Andean cosmology: *Uku Pacha, Kay Pacha,* and *Hanaq Pacha.* We were leaving the jungle, which represented *Uku Pacha,* the lower world of dense and heavy energy, symbolized by the snake and associated with transformation. I wondered whether it was a coincidence that I visualized the Kundalini serpent as rising within me during the ayahuasca ritual. In the *Uku Pacha,* we physically cleansed our body, facilitated by the plant medicine, before we traveled to the middle world, the *Kay Pacha,* our next destination.

Kay Pacha, the middle world inhabited by people, animals, and plants, was symbolized by the puma. For the next five days we would fly to Cusco (11,154 feet in altitude), take the train to Machu Picchu (7,874 feet in altitude), then, by bus, head to the Sacred Valley (altitude from 6,730–9,800 feet), visiting and doing ceremonies at the sacred sites.

In the higher altitudes, there is less atmosphere to absorb heat, so it's cooler. The ability of air to hold moisture is dependent on the temperature and the density of the atmosphere. At these higher altitudes, the air is thinner and drier with less concentration of oxygen and has a reduced ability to deliver oxygen and moisture to the tissues of the body. The organs of the body, such as the heart, lungs, and gastrointestinal tract, have to work harder for their oxygen. Symptoms of altitude sickness include shortness of breath, dizziness, nausea, fatigue, headaches, and difficulty sleeping. The short time that we were in Cusco allowed our bodies to partially acclimate prior to our descent to the relatively lower altitude of Machu Picchu in the Sacred Valley.

After the Sacred Valley, we would fly back to Cusco to catch a flight to La Paz, Bolivia (11,942 feet in altitude). We would then take a bus to our destination, Lake Titicaca, at 12,500 feet above sea level, where we would meet and do ceremony with the Indigenous community living in the highlands around the lake. This altitude represented *Hanaq Pacha*, the upper world, literally and figuratively. It was the realm of the spirit world and symbolized by the condor. That's where I would become blind.

May to October is wintertime in the southern hemisphere, opposite of the weather north of the equator. During the tour, the May weather ranged from midthirties to low sixties. Most of us had heard about altitude sickness but didn't worry that it might lead to death. A tourist in another group told me about her fellow traveler. "He took an antihistamine for his allergies. While the rest of us went exploring, he stayed on the bus because he was tired. When we got back, he was dead!" The lack of oxygen in the air at such a high altitude exacerbated the effects of the allergy medicine and suppressed his breathing to the point that he died while resting.

I had no medical conditions to limit me, but taking even ten steps at ten thousand feet left me short of breath. At the hotels, oxygen was available for those in obvious distress. For others, drinking coca tea or chewing coca leaves was recommended.

Although the coca plant has been equated with cocaine, there are up to fifteen other alkaloids that contribute to the biological activity of coca leaves with less euphoric effects than the isolated cocaine extract. At high altitudes, the lungs are not taking in as much oxygen as they are accustomed to, so the heart and lungs have to work harder to pump oxygen to the rest of the body. Chewing whole coca leaves or imbibing the tea decreases altitude sickness and suppresses hunger, thirst, pain, and fatigue. The benefits are from all the ingredients and not just the isolated cocaine extract. The tea has been compared to coffee in its action as a stimulant.

Wade Davis is a cultural anthropologist, ethnobotanist, author, educator, lecturer, photographer, and explorer. His work has focused on worldwide Indigenous cultures. In his YouTube lectures, he discusses the coca plant referenced in his 2009 book, *The Wayfinders: Why Ancient Wisdom Matters in the Modern World.* "And we did the first nutritional study of coca leaves. We found out that a small amount of cocaine hydrochloride, roughly ½–1 percent weight, roughly the amount of caffeine in a coffee bean, was absorbed orally when chewed. But in addition to the small amount of alkaloid absorbed benignly in the mucous membrane of the mouth, coca was chockful of vitamins. It had more calcium than any plant ever studied by science, which made it perfect for a diet that lacked a dairy product, particularly for mothers with infants. It also had enzymes in it which enhanced the body's ability to digest carbohydrates at high elevation, perfect for the tuber-based diet in the Andes. We showed that this plant that has been used with no evidence of toxicity, let alone addiction, for over eight thousand years by the people of the Andes." There are more than three thousand varieties of potatoes grown in the Andean highlands of Peru. What grew in nature helped the people of the Andes Mountain ranges to survive.

Coca tea was available in the hotels. The leaves were sold in the open-air markets, and tea bags were readily available in the local grocery stores. But the most effective cure for altitude sickness was descending toward sea level. I preferred drinking coca tea since the chewing process was more work. Chewing entailed breaking up the bitter leaves in my mouth along with a piece of lime (*llipta*), made of ashes of burnt seashells, limestone, or plants, that helped with the extraction of the alkaloids. Mixed with the saliva, a wad is formed that's placed on one side of the cheek, and the juices are absorbed through the oral mucosa throughout the day. Besides, the tea helped to keep me hydrated. However, I felt no improvement with my breathing even after constantly drinking coca tea and chewing the leaves. Just sitting and taking slow, deep breaths with no activity was the most comfortable, along with keeping hydrated.

Upon awakening on the first morning on the Bolivian side of Lake Titicaca, as I opened my eyes, the superficial layer of both corneas stuck to my upper eyelids and peeled off. My body was dehydrated, and overnight my eyelids stuck to the protective layer of my corneas. I had a history of dry eyes, and this had happened before when I visited friends living in the Arizona desert and sometimes during long flights. I always carried moisturizing eye drops but forgot to do so on this trip. The pain was overwhelming. The eyes have significantly more nerve receptors than skin since they process more information. Additionally, without the superficial coating, my eyes were susceptible to infection and more sensitive to the bright sun with less atmosphere to absorb and block the rays at such high altitude.

I was more irritated than alarmed that I would lose my vision. From past experience, I knew that the corneal surface of my eyes would regenerate in three days, but until then, I would have to wear sunglasses and open my eyes as little as possible while sightseeing and doing ceremony with the group. If I was at home, my ophthalmologist would have given me protective contact lenses or anesthetic eye drops, but in Bolivia I was lucky just to get eyedrops from one of the other travelers. I got around just by squinting but still couldn't get much relief with the constant irritation of the wind, cold weather, and bright sun. The most painful situation was a sacred ritual conducted by the Indigenous elders in the evening chill, sitting around a bonfire. Even with my eyes closed, I was sensitive to the alternating feeling of heat from the burning wood and the bone-chilling breeze. I imagined ashes whirling from the fire scattering in my direction. I protected my eyes as best as I could, enduring the pain because I didn't want to miss any of the experience.

On a pilgrimage like this, events were taken as omens, payback of karma incurred in the past, good or bad, and perhaps from another lifetime. If someone lost a souvenir, then that person was not supposed to have it, or it was not the amulet that he or she needed. If someone sprained an ankle, that person was not supposed to climb to sacred ground, or the injury might have occurred to prevent some danger up ahead. As I lost eyesight, either I was not supposed to experience certain landmarks or I was to rely on other senses. Or perhaps there was some other unknown, mysterious reason. All actions were the result of past actions and would impact future situations. We were exposed to a different way of thinking about life's experiences.

I pondered the spiritual significance of what I might have done in the past to incur my blindness, but it was burdensome to think about reciprocity for deeds bygone. Being from another culture, I took these situations as part and parcel of traveling and paid attention to present concerns. For those who lost a souvenir, a replacement could be purchased. For those who sprained an ankle, crutches or an arm of a friend would help them climb to see the sites. My suffering was limited; for the next three days, I continued to join my group conducting ceremony. Squinting through my sunglasses to the different locations, I was confident that within seventy-two hours my corneal abrasions would heal and my sight would be restored.

Transportation by airplane, train, and boat allowed movement through space and provided a type of time travel. It stimulated the neurons of the brain into new pathways of thinking. Experiencing foreign cultures that lived in accordance with nature, tasting their food, and seeing how they dressed lulled the senses and gave the illusion that boundaries of time had been erased.

Close to our hotel was an astronomy observatory. The last night on Lake Titicaca was the time we scheduled to observe the night sky, but the cloudy evening didn't allow for optimal stargazing, so Oscar arranged for an Indigenous elder to give coca leaf readings. He told us that the elder was in his midfifties but he looked like he was in his midseventies.

The elder sat cross-legged on the auditorium floor with his colorful poncho made of tightly woven wool tented over his frame. He wore an equally vibrant hat covering his head and ears with a fashionable pom-pom placed atop that shielded him from the chilly air of the unheated hall. The only visible motion was his outstretched right hand that threw dried coca leaves like dice on the floor in front of him and the slight movement of his lips as he mumbled in his native tongue.

One by one, we were called up to stand in front of the elder. Our guide sat next to him, interpreting for us. Those waiting stayed in their seats to allow privacy for the person being read. When it was my turn, I had no specific question and told our interpreter, "Please just ask him what he sees." Up close, I saw that the elder picked the most perfect of coca leaves from a bunch in front of him before tossing the chosen ones on the floor. All he said was, "You will be back soon."

That's it? I thought as I exited the auditorium. I was disappointed with the sparse statement, but then again, I hadn't given him a specific question. Three weeks of traveling and uprooting every couple of days was exhausting. *I may come back, but soon? Not likely.*

Three months later, I traveled back to South America, but it wasn't to Peru. My friend's husband wasn't able to make their scheduled trip, so she asked me if I wanted to take his place. I ended up sailing on an expedition to the Galápagos Islands. I had taken the Indigenous elder's vague prediction literally, as meaning that I would be coming back to Peru, but his statement could have just meant South America. He was close enough that I was a believer of his divination ability using what was common to his culture, coca leaves.

Chapter 16:

Miami: Refueling Stop

I returned to Florida to a lot of turmoil in my department. The newly graduated therapists thought they were going to run the inpatient and outpatient units, assuming my youthful appearance and short stature reflected inexperience and lack of leadership skills to direct patient care. The administrator of the physical medicine and rehabilitation department was always up in arms about something. There was always someone not doing what she wanted and not giving her enough credit. The doctors were not getting along.

I was intrigued by the Indigenous ceremonies and healing rituals in Peru and Bolivia. Here was a chance to integrate my two worlds. *See One. Do One. Teach One.* This was one of the memorable mantras that doctors-in-training would chant whenever faced with something new to learn. There was so much information to process. Repeating the short, precise commands infused us with confidence that it would be possible to grasp all aspects of a technique or subject as fast as we could repeat the syllables of the chant. I had seen the *curanderos* demonstrate clearing negative spirits from a ceremonial space several times. It seemed uncomplicated. I wanted to remove the negative energies in my workplace. I wanted to "do one." My experience with calling on spirits in my apartment was already forgotten.

I described the Peruvian ceremonies to the chief of my rehabilitation department and then asked permission to burn sage in our offices to clear the bad energy and promote harmony in our work spaces. I wasn't sure he believed that any plant medicine would drive egos and ambitions away, but being familiar with how grounded I was as a doctor and knowing that my intentions were in the right place, he allowed it. With a hearty laugh and a twinkle of amusement in his eyes, he said, "Go ahead. If you want to, you can take your clothes off, chant, and dance around naked." Humoring me, he added, "It can't hurt."

I laughed with him. I didn't mind that he was making light of my efforts. At least he was open to my trying alternative techniques to promote harmony in the workplace. It didn't interfere with my formal duties as a physician and I agreed, "It couldn't hurt."

After work, I burned sage in the different offices, with consent from the occupants, as well as my supervisor. I hoped to bring "love and light" to the environment and was careful not to set off smoke alarms.

In retrospect, my efforts to rid the department of discontent and competitive personality traits were in vain. Given the magnitude of this problem, the only thing that might have worked would have been applying the process used in termite elimination: tenting the hospital and fumigating the building for several days.

Despite the recent turmoil in my department, my situation in Miami Beach felt like a working vacation. I'd fallen into a happy rhythm working as a doctor and having time to study astrology. Iris held weekend classes and afterwards, I could go back to my own space and be comfortable. The thought of living in an ashram, taking care of a community, and being devoted to a guru did not appeal to me.

While traveling in the Galápagos Islands, I thought of the "survival of the fittest" phrase, made famous by naturalist Charles Darwin. While studying the wildlife of the islands, he made the observation that organisms that best adjusted to their environment had the most success in surviving and reproducing. He called this process of evolution "natural selection." I realized that if I had to survive in the forest or desert by myself, my DNA would have been selected out of the community gene pool very early on.

I couldn't travel living off the land. I didn't mind exploring in nature, but at night I had to have a door to lock, be able to take a shower, and have ready access to meals. My Mars ambition was geared more toward mental struggles than physical ones. I wanted time to think. I didn't want to spend all my energy trying to find food and shelter.

I attributed the way I traveled to Venus. Venus represented creativity, luxury, and beauty, as well as love and pleasure. Venus ruled the sign of Libra, and my second house was set in the sign of Libra. Taurus was on the cusp of my ninth house. Being owned by the same ruling planet linked the second house of money to the ninth house of long-distance travel and allowed me to travel in comfort.

The second house represented material possessions and resources, such as wealth needed to maintain survival, including food and family. Family was the initial means of sustenance. My parents gave me appreciation for a variety of different cuisines and stressed that nourishment was important to strengthen the body and mind. I liked good food.

To gain material wealth, learning marketable skills was necessary. Taurus's placement in the ninth house supported higher education, which was encouraged by my parents. Sensual Venus stoked my desire to experience different cultures firsthand, rather than just reading about them. The ninth house also signified the propensity for long-distance travel, which was how I wanted to learn. The Sun's placement in the ninth house supported growth in my educational endeavors. Mercury, residing with my Sun, allowed me to communicate what I'd learned. Educating patients and peers is part of being a doctor. Venus conferred creativity in the way I expressed information in venues such as lectures and publications.

I started looking at my horoscope not just as a diagram but as a series of interrelated pieces of information represented by the wheel of my chart divided into twelve sections. I started integrating information held by the different combinations of planets, houses, and signs placed in that circular chart, allowing me to speak the language of astrology more fluently.

My horoscope was the circle of my life with default settings. I couldn't change the initial setup of how I was programmed, but I could monitor transits, the ongoing movements of the planets, in contrast to their position at my birth.

In my birth chart, Saturn is positioned in the fifth house of Capricorn, putting limits in the areas of creativity, children, and romance. If I want to achieve progress in these sections of life, I will have to work hard to overcome obstacles. People with a heavy dose of Capricorn energy persevere and work hard to reach a goal. Saturn is the ruler of the sign of Capricorn. The sign and planet work in harmony. In my chart this combination manifests in a personality that doesn't mind working hard. I have the self-discipline to complete or reach a goal. Saturn provides lessons to learn, and through hard work one can reap the benefits he bestows. Even though I had doubts about completing my medical education, I persevered, and now had the freedom to travel and learn about different healing techniques.

My process of learning in astrology was similar to my medical training in that I needed to learn basic terms and principles before I could understand how they worked together, e.g., muscles are attached to each other but also to bone, and together they work to make a person walk or grab an apple. Eventually, the workings of the entire body were no longer a mystery.

Iris had said, "Astrology is not this chart; it's the interpretation." I was learning interpretation.

Over the next three years, I continued to study with Iris. I seldom socialized with her. Our meetings were in a class setting or a private reading. Despite the distance between us, we understood each other. Iris didn't need total devotion, and I respected the boundaries she set. She told me the best way to "use" her was to let her keep describing what she saw. "Let me keep talking. Don't interrupt me. Don't get too close. Then I'll be useless. My emotions will get in the way. I will start wanting to only see good circumstances for you. I won't be able to be objective." I listened to her and did not interrupt. In one session, my appointment went on for six hours, with her long monologue about how the United States will experience "enemies from within," the future of medicine for doctors, and how the brain will become more important in the future for healing. I would have let her go on, but we were interrupted by a phone call from my friend with whom I had plans for dinner. I had to leave.

After four years, I got tired of working at the Veterans Hospital, not because of patient care but because of maneuvering around administrative egotists who wanted recognition and control of the department. It took more effort than hospital duties.

During an annual appointment in 1999, Iris told me, "In a year, I don't see the VA. What's happening with you?"

"Well, the personalities at work are getting overbearing," I admitted. "I've had to strategize more when dealing with administration than patient care. I've been thinking about going to California, but I'm not sure what type of work would be available.

My father is getting really frail. He has diabetes, high blood pressure, and had heart surgery four years ago. It's hard flying back and forth to visit, but California's cost of living is so expensive."

Iris reassured me, "You'll be able to find work. You'll make enough. Anyhow, even if you just get a job, it'll be a transition period for you. You can look around, and after a year you're going to change jobs anyway." What she told me didn't mean anything to me at the time, but by then I was learning to listen to everything that she said, especially the casual remarks. Those often came to pass.

After medical training, my goal had been to find a practice, help build it, and work there until I retired. The Fort Myers job didn't turn out that way. Now, I found myself in another situation that had become unbearable because of personality issues.

A little less than a year prior to my move in May of 2001, an incident occurred that gave me more motivation to change my work situation. I'd held a morning meeting with the rehabilitation therapists to promote collegial interaction regarding patient care. In my naivete, I did not inform the department administrator because she didn't personally interact with patients. She marched into the meeting, breaking it up as if it were a drug bust. "What are you all doing here when there are patients waiting?" she thundered. "Everyone, get to work." She let everyone know that she was in charge.

I knew she was reacting this way because she wasn't the center of attention, the one calling the shots. She saw the meeting as my attempt to usurp her power. I rushed back to my office because I didn't want the team to see me cry at how I was being shamed. She didn't view my initiative as an effort to improve departmental communication.

After disbanding the team, the administrator opened the door to my office without knocking. In the confines of my office, I told her that it was a simple meeting I had scheduled to improve patient care, to try to communicate amongst the therapists and answer questions they had for me. I raised my voice at her as she tried to tell me I was totally wrong in not telling her. This was my Mars in defensive mode. There had been no malice toward her when I scheduled the team meeting. She was micromanaging our team and I felt her action to be unjust. I saw red and I couldn't think rationally. I just told her to get out of my office.

I continued to cry, not because I felt guilty about not informing her about the meeting but because it was a habit I couldn't control when expressing strong emotions, good or bad. I didn't like revealing my emotions in public. In a way, crying stopped me from blowing up. I strived for a pleasant, neutral doctor persona.

There was not a lot of discussion in my family. We weren't a vocally demonstrative family in terms of showing affection. The quiet hug would express joy or love. My parents showed their love through providing for their children, working hard to put food on the table, and enrolling us in school. It was when we strayed from appropriate behavior that my father would yell at us. If we talked back to a teacher or misbehaved on the school bus, that's when we got reprimanded. My parents were examples to their children of how to behave, and there was only a right and wrong way to act. There was no compromise. I was raised with the idea that no matter what was occurring in your personal life, you always presented a respectful public persona.

At the VA, I could treat veterans without checking to see if their insurance would cover their medical care. I didn't want to leave such a good job. This was a secure position, but I saw my behavior getting uglier in future dealings with administration and I couldn't allow my soul to fester in such an environment, regardless of how good the benefits might be. My dad's frail medical condition gave me a graceful reason to uproot.

I wanted to focus my Mars energy toward improving patient care and the creation of a harmonious work environment and not with strategic power struggles. Competitive ego combat was not constructive.

The last thing Iris told me in my 2000 reading was: "Follow your gut. If you don't change, change will still happen. Now, you have a choice."

By May of 2001, after five years of working and living in Miami, I had given my notice to resign. A colleague introduced me to her friend living in Berkeley, who hired me in a part-time capacity, and this friend found another physician who hired me for another part-time position. I was sad about leaving Miami. I had gotten so comfortable living on the beach but was ecstatic to leave my toxic work environment and be closer to my aging parents.

While packing up personal effects in my soon-to-be ex-office, I examined my business card with the VAMC logo embossed in black and shimmering gold. My business card declared me to be a medical doctor, but it wasn't all I wanted to be. Learning astrology with Iris had given me direction of what else I wanted to pursue, but because of distance I wouldn't be able to continue classes with her. Commuting from Oakland to Miami was not an option. It wasn't the Himalayas, but it was still a six-hour flight. Iris assured me I would meet many more practitioners, but I couldn't see that far ahead: I didn't have her vision. I was sad that my serious hobby would come to an end.

As much as I hated starting over in a new city, a new home, and a new job, I had to admit that my experiences in different cities, different cultures in the US and abroad, so far had exceeded anything that I had dreamed of as a child running after an airplane, wishing only to go to this far-off place, America.

Chapter 17:

What Does a Doctor Look Like?

In May of 2001, I moved from Miami to Oakland to work with two separate private medical practices. One job had me working primarily in Berkeley and the other was similar to my job in Fort Myers, necessitating a two-to-three-hour commute per day, subcontracting to several chiropractors and orthopedic practices in the Bay Area. It was exhausting.

The Bay Area was culturally diverse, with many people open to alternative medical treatments. Unfamiliar therapies were abundant and commonly advertised. If people believed in the healing benefits of a certain remedy and it wasn't authorized by their health insurance, most were willing to pay out of pocket. I wanted to seek and try out these alternative methods, but giving up the security of a job was not an option. Exploration had to wait until after I got established in the new area.

By November of 2001, I'd quit working as a subcontractor to work solely in the Berkeley practice, doing inpatient and outpatient care. In May of 2002, I quit the Berkeley position as well, not renewing my contract due to differing work philosophies. The medical environment in California was different than I was used to. Hospitals no longer billed for physicians since contracting with doctors was more cost-effective for the institutions. Just as Iris foretold, after a year I would be changing jobs and I would have no trouble finding work.

Two summers before I moved to California, the previously mentioned personality conflicts were starting to surface in my workplace in Miami. I drove back to the West Coast to see Jacy at the flea market, curious to see what she would say. Again, she saw that "in two weeks, two months, or two years," I was going to have "a major change." She explained that the number two was derived from my numerology. In addition to interpreting the tarot cards, she said, "I see you in front of computers."

"Well, medical records are getting transitioned from paper to electronic documentation, so I'm in front of the computer more."

Jacy elaborated, "No, what I get is that you will be paid to learn on a computer. Are you looking for a new job?"

"No, and I don't know of any job like that."

"Well, keep an open mind. It looks like a good situation, and it may come in two weeks, two months, or two years."

In January of 2002, two and a half years later, after having quit the first East Bay practice just a couple of months prior, I got administrative work as a medical consultant. My specialty in physical medicine and rehabilitation was well suited for work in chart review of musculoskeletal impairments, such as carpal tunnel syndrome and chronic back pain. This job required a six-month on-the-job training period to learn the regulations and computer programs. This must've been what Jacy had seen.

I wondered if six years ago Sam had seen Oakland when he saw California in my future. When there were long periods of time between the prediction and the event, it was hard to assess the prediction's validity, but Sam did say he wasn't sure about the timing of some of the events he saw.

Iris told me that she wasn't guarded in what she would tell me about future events because she knew I wouldn't forsake present responsibilities to wait for good fortune to just happen. If opportunities presented themselves, it was because of the choices I made along the way. She told me, "If you improve your character, you improve your destiny." I had to leave Miami Beach because I couldn't let the toxic environment adversely change me.

One night in early spring of 2002, driving home from work in rush-hour traffic heading south on Interstate 80, just as I passed the 99 Ranch Market between the cities of El Cerrito and Albany, I started seeing an image in the space about a foot in front of me. I could only explain it as a mirage that stayed in front of my visual field even as I moved my head. The moving image was highlighted in the background of the darkening early evening sky.

I was having a vision. All I'd had to drink that day was coffee and caffeinated soda. I'd never had this experience before. I recognized Leonardo da Vinci's *Vitruvian Man*, enclosed in a circle and a square, clearly visible in 3D. His outstretched limbs were moving like the hands of a clock and pointing to different astrological signs instead of numbers. The symbols were quivering as they revolved in a circle. The glyph of Gemini, my astrological sign, kept vibrating more prominently than the other symbols.

I reminded myself to be present and watch the traffic. The animation moved wherever my gaze went, competing with the heavy traffic for my attention. With no chance of exiting onto the frontage road due to the congestion, I focused my eyesight, alternating on the traffic and the moving image, trying to decipher the reason for the apparition and hoping for safety during my drive. Talking to no one in particular, I kept saying, "Whoever is doing this, this is not a good time."

By the time I passed Bay Street Mall in Emeryville, my breathing had normalized. The vision, which lasted about two minutes, was long gone, but I was still a bit shaken as to what had happened. Then, I thought about the unseen entities with whom I'd made a deal as a child. They continued to honor my request by not appearing to me when awake, but they cheated. They showed an image instead, to communicate a message in a situation where I had heightened awareness.

I got home safely and contemplated what I'd seen: the *Vitruvian Man* with his outstretched limbs in two superimposed positions, simultaneously enclosed in a circle, and a square representing "The proportions of the human body according to Vitruvius." Da Vinci combined science (geometry, symmetry) and art with the practice of medicine in this simple drawing. He had dissected corpses to familiarize himself with the human body to more accurately depict it in the figure.

I interpreted the message as man being represented by the horoscopic wheel of astrology, recognizing the circle and astrological symbols enclosing the human figure. I couldn't explain the square, though. I saw the communication as a sign to continue studying astrology and to connect it with my profession.

However, I kept my priorities: day job first, then astrology.

I enjoyed my administrative work. I didn't have to drive to different locations. There were no medical emergencies. It was a collegial atmosphere. I had many discussions with the head of my division, Dr. James, whose specialty was neurology. He was close to twenty years older than me and liked to be called by his first name. James liked people. He liked talking and getting to know all the administrative staff, not just the medical personnel. After discussing cases, conversations would often wander into topics other than medicine, like food or movies. He was well-read and talked about many subjects freely. I felt comfortable speaking my mind, even to criticize his views on any topic, and vice versa.

During lunch one afternoon, Dr. James and I had a long conversation about how lucky we were to find this job at a time when restrictions were being placed on the clinical time we could spend with outpatients. We compared and commiserated on the current politics of our chosen career. To receive reimbursement for clinical services, doctors had to pay more attention to the flood of paperwork mandated by the insurance companies than to patients. Working part-time in clinical medicine, I complained about being limited to thirty minutes per patient, which didn't include documentation time. This environment motivated both of us to look for a less complicated way to practice medicine. In my part-time practice in Berkeley, I'd applied to be a provider for the Medi-Cal health-care program. After one year of seeing patients, I was reimbursed with two fifteen-cent checks. It would have been more profitable to ask for the postage as payment.

Then, James mentioned that luck followed him throughout his career. I told him, "You're smart, but it helps that you're a man." Some of Dr. James's experience with medical training sounded like a fairy tale. My friend, being well over six feet with the most pleasant, conversational demeanor, aced his surgical rotation without spending time in the operating room. Endowed cerebrally with book smarts, he viewed all the blood and gore of surgery to be appalling manual labor and wanted no part of the tedious work. "I didn't want to be a surgeon. I didn't see the need to go through the rotation."

James devised a plan to avoid being in the operating room. He knew of another student whose ambition was to spend as much time in the operating room (OR) as he could, and this student agreed to take his place during surgeries. James rationalized, "We were the same height, and when gown and mask were donned, how could anyone tell?"

He bragged, "I got the highest grade on the surgery exam, but only got an A for the rotation. I was so annoyed." My lucky friend could not bury his indignation, so he marched into the chief surgeon's office and boldly asked why he didn't get an A+. "I did, after all, get the highest grade on the test."

"Yes," the chief explained, "but no one remembers you ever being in the OR."

With that comment, Dr. James retreated, bright enough not to push his luck.

As much as we were able to speak freely, I couldn't tell him about my own surgical rotation experience; I was still ashamed to have fallen short of my expectations as a medical student, fifteen years earlier.

The surgical field was competitive. Students wanting to go into the field of general surgery and surgical subspecialties usually picked surgery as their first rotation in the fourth year of medical school, since it allowed them to get recommendations, apply, and be accepted early for residency programs. And if they were not accepted by their first choice, they still had the time to apply to their second and third choices.

I got stuck with surgery as a first rotation because I delayed ranking preferences; I didn't know what specialty I wanted to enter after medical school. General surgery was the only option available to me. I never aspired to be a surgeon. To top it all off, I had to repeat this surgical rotation because the senior resident assumed that I wanted to be a surgeon without ever asking me. In his opinion, I was not worthy to become a surgeon.

As a female doctor, I wanted to be knowledgeable and professional, with a polished look. My mother wanted me to do well in training but also to "look like a doctor." She worked as a nurse, educated in the Philippines, in the age when the dress code was crisp, starched, and ironed white uniforms with white stockings and low-heeled shoes, topped off with a winged nurse's cap to complete the advertised stereotype of nursing personnel. During World War II, Mom joined the Philippine Air Force to become a flight nurse. She met my aunt in school, who then introduced her to my father.

All the images from her tour of duty were taken by professional photographers, so the pictures in Mom's photo albums all showed figures in their best outfits, whether in uniform or casual attire. Even the candid shots were orderly and showed well-kept individuals. She wanted me to look like that all the time, and it had an impact on me.

In medical school, I wore skirts and stockings because I wanted to look professional while wearing my sterile white lab coat—my superhero cape—which undeniably announced me as a doctor. During surgical rotation, I continued to wear heels and stockings, even knowing that procedures could last more than six to eight hours. My styled hairdo and full makeup, hidden by the operating room cap and mask, mattered only to me. That's what I thought.

Apparently, my supervising resident noticed. I didn't act or look like a surgeon. I was thrust into this surgical rotation with testosterone-driven, male would-be surgeons, whose immediate goal was to crush the competition and secure their future with a spot in any surgical program. To hell with altruism. That would come later.

In my senior surgical resident's estimation, I didn't have the aggression or the knowledge to make it. The rotation was my first foray into the bloody arena. The thought of using a scalpel to cut any flesh was horrifying. Also, I was sensitive to the smells of burning flesh from the cauterization used to stop bleeding. I got nauseous and the bright lights overhead gave me headaches. I had to stand on two step stools to reach the operating table set at the height for the attending surgeon. I was in a cockfight with masked gladiators who made it clear I would not survive. All these factors contributed to my having to repeat the rotation.

Rejected and dejected, I decided to turn in my superhero cape. I informed my guidance counselor that I was going to quit medical school. The head of the medical school called me in. I was not allowed to fail. He told me, "The state put a lot of funds into your education. You've come so far. I'm going to set you up with a psychiatrist."

The psychiatrist understood and commiserated with my situation, but she didn't tell me anything I didn't already know. "Medicine is stressful. It's just a small setback. You're almost at the end." I wanted her to say, "Okay, you're a hard worker. We'll let you pass." Instead, she gave me an antidepressant and a follow-up appointment. The first pill made me more sedated and prone to wallow in self-disappointment with the dread of everyone knowing I failed the rotation. I never took another pill, and I never went back for the follow-up appointment.

My parents came to visit me, not to stop me from quitting school but to see how I was doing. They wanted to talk to me and give me some support for whatever decision I'd make. They knew that I was working very hard and that medical school was difficult.

I thought Dad would push the issue of finishing school, but he didn't. He didn't tell me that I would only have to repeat three months and that I had come so far. Instead, he told me a story that he'd never mentioned before. For the first five years of being in the United States, no one talked to him at work. He was the only person who was dark-skinned in the mechanical engineering department of US Steel Corporation. On top of that, he had a thick accent. He just continued to do his work. It was the only thing he could do. He endured for his family's future.

When he spoke, he expressed no anger or resentment. It was like it was another person he was describing. He had transcended the experience because he was able to provide for his family and we had done well.

The situation changed after five years, when my brothers and some of his coworkers' sons were in the same tennis league. My brothers and the coworkers' children communicated through sports with no thought of skin color. That's when the other parents started talking to my father, seeing him in a different light.

My immigrant parents showed me by example that persevering through obstacles was a way to improve life. I had work to do. I got through my shame, repeated my rotation, and even scored high on the surgical exam. Even so, I only got a *pass* on my transcript. It took all the courage I had to make an appointment with the chief surgeon of the department to ask why. He looked at me with disdain and said, "You took the rotation twice. You had more time to study." There was no discussion, no encouragement. He dismissed me by asking, "Is there anything else?"

James had more stories about his good fortune. He described that even a caustic evaluation of his overall medical school performance was not an obstacle to being accepted at a prestigious program. He had applied for a six-month neurology elective in London at Queen Square Institute of Neurology, and the recommendation letter from the vice chair of the medical department described him as "irresponsible and incompetent" based on his "lackadaisical attitude." Later, the interviewers in London told him, "They never said you were stupid." They told my friend, "We had a bit of a laugh and said we must meet this man." James got the position and thoroughly enjoyed his rotation.

I asked James if he knew anything about astrology.

"I had a reading once and was told I was a Libra with Libra rising. I don't remember much else. After that I read some of Dane Rudhyar's books on the subject. Extremely insightful," he replied.

"He's very philosophical, but he's a hard read for me," I said. "I had to think about every sentence before I could go on to the next."

Libra's an air sign that describes those who are intellectual and devoted to abstract and theoretical points of view, rather than concrete, hands-on duties like surgery. It made for good neurologists who can go through complex thought processes as they consider the differential diagnoses of neurological impairments. James's mind retained minutiae. He could easily spout off differential diagnoses and treatments for specific neurologic diseases, sometimes ad nauseum. At times, I'd interrupt to tell him to stop giving me a lecture. He took no offense. He just ignored me and continued with his train of thought. No feathers were ruffled. Although I missed patient care, the administrative job was less stressful with easygoing colleagues like James, and I could take time to travel when I wanted.

Libra is symbolized by the balanced scales. Because James got a double dose, born under the sign of Libra (September 23–October 22) with the same constellation rising in the east at the time of his birth, he had balance in excess. He could see both sides of an argument to such a degree that he could be indecisive.

In one instance, after trying to train a physician applicant on the computer system at work, I told James that the candidate was not able to catch on to the electronic setup, and as a result I recommended that the candidate wasn't a good hire. James kept telling me to train him. "I want to give him every chance to get a job." Of course, he wasn't the one doing the training.

After another two weeks, I went into James's office again and told him that I hadn't gotten far in going over the agency regulations since the candidate needed to be cued on all aspects of using the programs, such as clicking onto the next screen. I repeated, "The trainee will never be independent in the computer system." Not wanting to make the call to dismiss the applicant, James asked an administrative supervisor for a second opinion on the physician. In less than one hour, the doctor was let go.

Libras are concerned with acceptance by peers, and for that reason, they see all sides of an issue. They want to be accommodating to everyone. So, it made sense that everyone liked James and wanted to accommodate him, liked to help him. He didn't have to try hard to accomplish goals. He was the perfect diplomat, well suited to be the head of the medical team at the office, mediating between medical and administrative personnel who sometimes had differing views on how to achieve the same objectives.

We had similar personalities. We both liked to be pleasant and accommodating, but James's genetics allowed him to fly through hoops I stumbled over in the same environment, because he fit the stereotypical image of a doctor.

What helped me get through training was my Taurean determination to get an education and my Martian aggression modified by a pleasant Gemini flexibility. I had luck too. Jupiter was in my fifth house of service and enemies, but a lackadaisical demeanor didn't work for me. I'd always had to be professional. I cultivated serious competence.

While working at the VA, I worked better when invisible. I was self-assured and commanding when talking to my colleagues on the phone. No one pushed me around, but face-to-face, I undermined myself. I felt my taller, mostly male colleagues sizing me up. Being short and a woman of color, I looked at myself through their eyes, my mother's words coming back to me: "You don't look like a doctor."

Mom grew up in a different time. The vintage pictures in her album showed women who were making their mark. They were proud to be nurses in the Philippine Air Force during World War II and wanted to show strength in their femininity.

In medical school, I wasn't trying to make a mark as much as trying to find my way. I watched how strong women around me bypassed obstacles, and I looked to them for strategies during this stage of my development. I envied them. I took notes to learn how to think and act like them.

My friend Abby, from New Jersey, was tall, blond, and not easily intimidated. She also was the only female in her surgical rotation. She told me that the attending surgeon would give each training doctor a turn to make the first incision. Abby explained, "It's usually the person closest to him. He let the group decide who would be on the right-hand side of God."

She told me, "The men in the group made a pact. They would take turns." They planned to crowd Abby out, keep her in the back. She would never get the scalpel. But the guys were not getting away with it. They had forgotten about the other women in the room.

Once everyone was gloved and gowned, the attending surgeon signaled the start of the procedure with a single word, "Knife." It was the surgical nurse's cue to pick up the tool and hand it to the resident closest to him. One time, however, she slowly circled to the back of the pack and handed the coveted instrument to Abby.

"Heh, heh, well, boys, make room for the surgeon." With the attending's chuckle, the operation began.

Abby had gone to the nurse before the surgery began, explaining, "These guys are trying to screw me over. Could you please give me the scalpel when we start?"

While training at the Veterans Hospital, with its high percentage of male patients and female nurses, I learned about cultivating a diplomatic but firm bedside manner from a female senior surgical resident. I made a mental note to copy her no-nonsense professional behavior.

As we were making rounds, checking on patients to see how they were progressing, one crusty patient complained to the senior resident, "Doctor, I'm having trouble peeing; I need a straight cath." This procedure required the caregiver to insert a tube manually, from the head of the penis to the bladder, bypassing any obstruction to urine flow. However, this patient did not have any history of urinary issues.

Without a beat, the resident replied, "The nurses are changing shifts right now, but Jerry, the nursing assistant, will be happy to help you. He's a Vietnam vet, and he'll take good care of you."

Our group left the room showing no disrespect to the patient and preventing harassment of the female nursing staff. I chuckled to myself and looked back at the patient's wide-eyed, open-mouth stare, knowing that Jerry would not be asked to help him. Best of all, I was sure that the person's difficulty with urination was resolved without further treatment.

As my clinical education progressed, I got more comfortable with my work and a more practical, disheveled appearance. Working more than ninety hours in the hospital was a short week and didn't include studying. To be presentable, bathing and wearing clean underwear became the only necessity. My mother would look at me horrified, asking, "How would anybody know that you're a doctor?"

I understood Mom's point of view and I took no offense, since I knew she was proud and supported my efforts. I would tell her, "When I'm working, I can't be all dressed up. I'm still a doctor, no matter what I look like." This statement seemed to mollify her concerns. This was my time, and I was making my own traditions. My rumpled, superhero cape had started flapping in the wind.

Chapter 18:

Vedic Astrology

"Hi, everyone! Why don't we all introduce ourselves? Just your name and where you're from." Class had begun—again—for me in San Rafael. One of many, and with different teachers. Iris was right; I'd been able to find more resources to continue my study of astrology. I heard about east Indian or Vedic astrology from a colleague at the administrative office. She gave me her extra copy of *Light on Life: An Introduction to the Astrology of India* by Hart de Fouw and Robert Svoboda. It was a book of Jyotish or Vedic astrology. It was a comprehensive and detailed introduction to the rules of astrology from the authors' study of Sanskrit texts and the knowledge imparted by their teacher.

It was the handbook for life that I'd been searching for during medical training. I didn't recognize the reference material at first since I'd decided long ago that such a manual didn't exist, but as it turned out, I just had to wait until it was written. It wasn't easy reading with its use of Sanskrit terms and different concepts, but the text mirrored the complexities of life. By the time that I moved to the Bay Area, there were many such handbooks and not limited to astrology. There was a market for these texts. From the classes I attended, it seemed that many other people besides me had been looking for them.

The Western astrology that I learned from Iris uses the tropical system. This zodiac is centered around the movement of the Sun and coincides with the seasons: the sign of Aries is associated with spring (March 21–April 19), Cancer coincides with the start of summer (June 21–July 22), Libra is assigned to the fall season (September 23–October 22), and the sign of Capricorn ends the year during winter (December 22–January 19).

Vedic astrology uses the sidereal system. The dates of the zodiacal signs correspond to the actual location of the constellation in which the Sun is situated in the sky. The Earth rotates on a tilted axis, and with the gravitational pull of the Sun and Moon the equatorial area bulges, causing the tilted axis to wobble during its revolution around the Sun, similar to the fanning out of a skater's skirt as she spins.

To illustrate this, imagine your head is the Earth and tilt it to the right to simulate the angulation of Earth's axis. Sit on a chair that swivels and spin around in a circle. It's hard to keep your head at the same slant because of the centrifugal force, the acceleration that acts outwardly away from the center of rotation. With the sway of your head, the direction of your gaze is changed slightly, even though your head has the same slant.

This is similar to what happens to Earth because of the gravitational pull of the Sun and Moon on the equator. This wobble or precession doesn't change Earth's tilt, but the orientation changes. Every 26,000 years, the direction that the Earth's rotational axis points to in the sky makes one complete revolution, a circle, so that the axis does not point exactly in the same direction, shifting the view of the sky.

The sidereal calendar system takes into account this wobble, such that the Sun is viewed in the constellation of Aries from April 14–May 14, in Cancer from July 16–August 16, in Libra from October 17–November 15, and in Capricorn from January 14–February 12.

I likened the differences between these two interpretations, between the Western and Vedic systems, as similar to the medical subspecialties' point of view of the body. In general, neurologists treat the electrical system of the body. The cardiologist is concerned with heart function. The gastroenterologist makes sure that the body's ability to absorb nutrients and excrete waste products functions normally. My physical medicine and rehabilitation specialty deals with optimizing the function of muscles and nerves to improve quality of life. The physicians in the subspecialties place their emphasis on different organs but are aware that the function of all the tissues is interrelated. No organ functions in isolation. Together they comprise the human body, with each specialty having a specific point of view.

Whether viewed from a Western tropical or Vedic sidereal point of view, the science regarding the planets, the constellations, and the characteristics assigned to them is similar in both Western and Vedic astrology. Regardless of whether tropical or sidereal astrology is used, the planets, Sun, and Moon have the same positions relative to each other in the sky. The subtleties in interpretation reflect differences in the mythology and traditions of the culture from which the system originated. I was still the same person no matter which system described me.

The Vedic classes started with the same basic information. The teacher explained, "The zodiac describes the path of the Earth, Moon, Sun, and the planets with respect to the twelve constellations." He continued, "If you were to look on the eastern horizon on the date and time of your birth, the constellation that you would see is your rising or ascending sign. The stories associated with this group of stars would describe how the world sees you— the personality that you project to the world. A person with Aries rising would be a go-getter, ambitious in some way. Home would be important to someone with Cancer rising."

One newbie asked, "Then why are people who are born on the same date and time different?"

"Location, location, location. A person living in Moscow, born at the same time as a person living in Lima, will see different constellations along their respective eastern horizons." A Confucius-like reply followed. "Surroundings also play a role. Just as a rose thrives in temperate weather, it will wither in the desert. But anything can thrive if it receives the appropriate care, in any climate. Environment also includes social circumstances, educational opportunities, and financial status."

Then the teacher started drawing the horoscope. The Vedic system uses a square horoscope with intersections creating twelve triangular and diamond-shaped spaces. The image of the *Vitruvian Man* flashed in my mind, with the circle and the square enclosing him. Could the circle represent Western astrology and the square represent the Vedic system? My interpretation of my vision was that the proportions of man could be interpreted from both the Western and Vedic astrological systems.

He continued, "The planets have assigned personalities and duties. The goddess Venus is known for beauty and is associated with fine arts, while the masculine god Mars is generally linked with war and aggressive behavior. The Sun represents life-giving energy, and sometimes the man in the Moon can be seen." He was being dramatic about how imagination works.

I just wanted the facts and to learn how the Vedic system approached interpretation. Instead of Greek and Roman mythology of gods and goddesses, I was transported into Indian lore of devas and demons, larger-than-life beings with human qualities of lust and greed, as well as compassion and intellect—ancient versions of soap operas.

The teacher continued, "Numerous fairy tales were handed down from generation to generation in oral tradition describing perils and adventures which applied to daily mortal life—all with lessons to learn. Embellishments captured the imagination, and stories made it easier to remember instructions."

I knew for a fact that vivid imagery facilitated learning. I thought back to a coarse but memorable lesson I'd learned from a solid, son-of-a-gun general surgeon who'd stressed the importance of the rectal exam in a complete history and physical evaluation of every male patient. He emphasized that diagnosing prostate or rectal cancer was worth the perceived violation.

He looked at each of us students in the eye and, in his own gruff, Confucius-like manner, declared, "You do the patient a disservice if you exclude this practice. There are only two reasons why you don't do a rectal exam: one, if your patient doesn't have an anus, and two, if you don't have a finger."

I started taking Vedic astrology classes in San Rafael sporadically, in between work. The basic classes weren't being offered, but I wanted to learn more about the subject, so I signed up for available courses. In one advanced class, my ears perked up when someone asked, "Can a chart show homosexuality?"

Okay, this should be interesting!

Whether embryos have the genetic makeup of XX (female) or XY (male) chromosomes, during early development all fetal (an embryo becomes a fetus at eleven weeks of pregnancy) genitalia are undifferentiated and are phenotypically (by outward appearance) female. If the hormone testosterone isn't produced, a baby girl develops.

Is the identity orientation due to biology, a glitch in the genetic translation for chemical production, and/or due to environmental factors at the time of early human development?

Medical astrology is a specialized field that can show the tendencies for almost any physical ailment, whether musculoskeletal, gastrointestinal, neurological, or cardiac. Could the inclination for gender or sexual preference be seen in the astrological chart?

The astrology teacher described a personal experience he'd had: "I had a client, young, attractive. He wanted a relationship, but he couldn't make a connection in his dating life. Trying to help him out, I told him to put an ad in the paper saying that his astrologer, me, would check every applicant's chart for compatibility, and that's how he would pick a date."

Everyone in the class laughed at such an offer, an early version of computerized matchmaking. Genius! If only he had the foresight to market this idea! I wished that I were the lucky client.

"Never again!" the teacher promised. "Over thirty women responded! But I kept my word. I found three people I felt would be compatible with him. Years later he came back and explained that the dates didn't work out. Somewhere along the way, he figured out he was gay. So, no, there is no specific astrological combination that points to sexual preference—that I know of."

I figured the code just hadn't been broken yet. Answers still might be held in the position of planets at the time of birth. As an example, look at DNA, the blueprint of life. It took a while, but now the human gene can be sequenced, read, and manipulated.

More research just needed to be done. It was information. When treating patients, you try to get as much information as you can to help them. For example, when someone comes into the emergency room for chest pain, the patient is interviewed about what his activities had been, what foods he had eaten. What kind of medication(s) had he taken? Any recent substance abuse or trauma? Anyone who comes with the patient is interviewed. Diagnostic tests are done looking for abnormalities to isolate what body system(s) could be causing the pain complaints. The etiology of the pain complaints could be from a simple muscle strain when lifting weights or from a spicy meal, and not from the heart. Information helps to clarify the mystery of a patient's symptoms, but not everything in the realm of man is to be explained, in medicine or astrology, such as the etiology of sexual preference/orientation.

I don't feel that astrology can explain how the human body functions absolutely, but I feel that it can be used as an adjunct to help clarify tendencies in the twelve areas of life, including the tendency to manifest certain medical conditions. Astrology is a different method for interpreting information. The interpretation of the horoscope is a theory of how the planets, Sun, and Moon describe human behavior and condition. Curiosity must be explored. If questions aren't asked, then answers can't be found. Inventions can't be discovered. New uses for old discoveries won't be conceived. For example, botulinum toxin, commonly known as Botox, helps relax muscles. Injections are administered to decrease spastic muscle stiffness, spasms, and contractions in patients with cerebral palsy, blepharospasms (uncontrolled blinking), and cervical dystonia (severe neck spasms), to name a few impairments. Botulinum toxin is relatively safe, as it tends to have a local and not systemic action. It can remain active in the target area for four to six months. It has been found to be useful in smoothing out wrinkles and therefore has been popularly repurposed for off-label use in the cosmetic field.

In class, everyone listened intently, trying to get a handle on the rules, listening for the information that applied to them. That's how you learn best—when the rules apply to you. In class, we all had some issues we wanted worked out. After getting my medical degree, I thought my life would lead to marriage and children. My curiosity led me to studying astrology, which helped me see the strengths and weaknesses in my life and that I had choices other than what society expected.

We all wanted reassurance that the path we were on was the right one. Like me, my fellow students were looking for information to help them understand themselves and the specific situations of life in which they were living. Astrology might help to bypass difficulties in life or see options that were not obvious. Given a map, who wouldn't look for detours and bridges that would bypass or ameliorate the obstacles of life? Nobody I knew.

Chapter 19:

Remember What We Forgot

It'd been two years since I left Miami, but Iris-isms, things she said about me or phrases that seemed to have a universal truth, kept coming to mind. "You're never going to stop learning. You'll always want to learn."

Some people keep up with fashion trends, monitor the stock market, or watch for what is hot in the culinary world. The Gemini in me likes to collect all sorts of information. If Saturn the disciplinarian didn't focus me, I could be very scattered in my interests, flitting from subject to subject. A part of me wanted to be content with being a Western doctor, but the radar of my ninth house of higher education always looked for different trends in the subject of health. Practical Saturn gave me a good occupation, allowing me to pursue my interests independently.

I was glad that I'd moved out West. The job prospects were better in the Bay Area than in Southern California and offered much more convenient travel to see my parents in San Diego than Miami. During a weekend visit with them, the image of Rosita Arvigo in a Sunday newspaper magazine caught my eye.

Her book *Sastun* was featured. A *sastun* is a sacred object that assists a shaman in his work. *Sastun* offered a glimpse into her teacher, Don Elijio Panti, and his Belizean practice. The picture alongside the article showed a slender figure dwarfed by the background of a lush green rain forest that was her home office. She had soft brown eyes, a curly mop of dark hair, and a prominent jaw. Scanning the photograph, I looked at her eyes, trying to get a glimpse into the personality of someone who would move from the city jungle of Chicago to an actual jungle.

It was 2002 and ethnobotany, the study of the relationship between plants and man, was a prevalent topic associated with saving the rain forest, the origin of most modern prescription medicines. In the article, Rosita stressed that preservation of the tropical environments was necessary as they harbored the fundamental elements for curing ailments yet untreated, like cancer. The healers, the guardians with knowledge of medicinal properties of the plants catalogued in their memories, were aging, and most had no students willing to learn the old ways. The wisdom from the past would be lost with their passing.

I was interested in exploring the customs and beliefs from my own Philippine background, but the opportunities were not easily accessible and safety was a concern. That year there had been a magnitude-7.5 earthquake in Mindanao, kidnappings, as well as bombings in Zamboanga City near a karaoke bar, a candle store at a Catholic shrine, and a shopping center.

When I was younger and first expressed my interest in the medical field, my father would tell me he would take me back to the Philippines, to the places he knew from his childhood, including the remote areas where psychic surgery was being performed. He also described that people would come from all over to visit and get remedies from his aunts. I loved the plan. I could understand Tagalog and Ilocano but couldn't speak the languages well enough to get around by myself. My dad would have been the perfect travel guide. But after so many years, the familiar faces my father knew were gone. By the time I finished medical training, got settled with a stable job, and had the time and finances to make the trip, Dad was in his eighties, in poor health, and travel was not possible for him.

Any topic dealing with medical care, especially coming from Indigenous healers, fascinated me. These local granny healers, midwives, and shamans relied only on their knowledge and experience of what treatments had worked in the past. They had no access to diagnostic technology to aid their medical skills. They had no X-rays that showed where broken bones were splayed or laboratories that analyzed any imbalance in the chemical composition of blood. I was determined to meet Rosita and to learn firsthand what she knew.

In medical school, reading textbooks was a necessity to gain familiarity with all aspects of a topic. Reading instructions in a manual was one-dimensional and unemotional, but to achieve great skill when doing medical procedures, there was absolutely no substitute for the actual experience, like doing surgery. Once you hold a scalpel in your hand and start cutting into flesh, you start feeling compassion and responsibility for this patient who is a human being and hoping that you can do your best to help them. You also don't want to make any mistakes in front of your mentors. The surgical procedure is no longer just a theory when you feel the warm tissues through your gloved hands while watching blood as it oozes from each incision you make. You smell the constant smoke and burnt flesh from the Bovie, the electrocautery tool used to achieve hemostasis, to control the constant bleeding that occurs with each slice of the scalpel. There is anxiety and exhilaration that you are actually cutting into a person and not just a cadaver.

I read *Sastun* within a month of the featured article. The book recounts many stories of discovery, describing the different medicinal plants used and the prayers beckoning the spirits to aid their efforts while treating patients. Next, I wanted to meet the person and get to know the character of a woman who would uproot from the security of a familiar city lifestyle to unknown encounters with a shaman in the jungle, for an education. I wanted to know the old ways. The Taurus in me had a romantic vision of Rosita's training as described in *Sastun* and wanted a sensual adventure: to pick the sacred plants, smell skunk root, taste the bitterness of the healing herbs, hear the sounds of the jungle, and sweat in its humidity. I wanted to experience Rosita's journey. *Sastun* was to be my primer and, I made up my mind, the Belizean rain forest would be my operating room, somehow.

An opportunity to meet Rosita came a few months later. She would be teaching Maya Abdominal Therapy, which she had learned from Don Elijio Panti. I traveled to a rural area of Massachusetts where Rosita was offering a weekend workshop concentrating on self-care techniques in women's health. It was the first in an abdominal massage series she was teaching. Rosita was making sure that the world did not forget the old ways.

The twenty participants, along with Rosita, stayed at The Round House, a fourteen-sided, four-storied building that had thirty individual beds in either curtained cubbies or bedrooms. The bottom floor had a large open area with ample space for us to sit on rugs, cushions, or chairs during the lectures. When it was time for the hands-on massage work, half of us could lie down comfortably while the other half practiced on us.

As a doctor who specialized in musculoskeletal injuries, I'd learned to locate spasms and tightness in the superficial skeletal muscles but was having trouble locating the positions of the more deeply located ovaries and uterus with the massage. I had abdominal scars sustained from the moving vehicle accident when I was eight. As I'd been hit from behind, the exploratory laparoscopy revealed many internal injuries, and I was left with a nine-inch midline abdominal scar. For most of my three-month stay in the hospital, I urinated from a tube exiting on the right side of my abdomen to allow my kidney lacerations to heal. On the back of my right thigh, I had a permanent dent the width and size of the fender that hit me. The thigh muscle never filled out, but since I was young when injured, the other leg muscles were able to accommodate my injury as I got older. I walked normally and had no limitations with activities such as running.

Rosita was very open about her experiences when talking about Don Elijio Panti and how she wanted to spread the sacred plant medicine and the Indigenous healing techniques she'd learned, especially concerning women's health. By doing weekend seminars in the United States, Rosita was able to disseminate the information.

Rosita's curly hair had touches of gray that weren't present in her Sunday circular picture. She wasn't as outgoing as I thought she'd be. She and her family had moved to Belize in the 1980s to live closer to the land, and I imagined that since 1994, when *Sastun* was published, she'd been teaching and traveling. Pondering her situation, I could understand that after eight years this routine of meeting so many people could wear you out and after a while you just want to do your work and retreat to a quiet place when done. She socialized only with people she was familiar with, and unless you had a medical question, she was distant. She was focused on spreading the teaching. Once she did her lectures, she and her assistants went around overseeing our techniques. For the most part, Rosita was all business. She had started grooming trainers to carry on the education when she couldn't, so that the Maya teachings would not be lost—a lesson she'd learned from Don Elijio's situation.

I decided to just learn what she had to offer, a little deflated from my expectation of having an open discussion about her experiences as described in *Sastun*, but I understood as I had been in the same situation of teaching medical personnel and students. It's hard to give every student individual attention, and all you can hope for is to accomplish your instructional goals, especially for a weekend intensive with twenty students.

Rosita instructed, "Lie down in a flat but comfortable position. Using the belly button as the center, with the fingertips of both hands apply a gentle but forceful and deep pressure from each of the four corners of the abdomen toward the belly button. Repeat for about ten minutes."

Under my fingertips and hands, all I felt was the soft consistency of a dense foam cushion and no distinct organ structures. This process reminded me of when I tried to learn Braille and found that my fingertips were not as sensitive to the closely spaced bumps on the paper to even start the association of nubs to the alphabet.

As all the students did the self-massage, Rosita continued, "This basic process helps loosen the internal tissues and all the organs in the abdomen—not just the reproductive ones. It allows the organs to move more freely. Results vary depending on what the person's medical issues are. For some, the process helps promote intestinal propulsion, treating constipation. Others will see an improvement in their menstruation patterns."

I did not have the dramatic results that some people in the group experienced, but there seemed to be no harm in the method. The process of stretching tissues in a gentle manner made sense to me. Flexibility is important for good health and function of the superficial skeletal muscles as well as the internal tissues. I planned to continue the massage on myself.

At the end of the long weekend session, Rosita mentioned she'd be holding another workshop in Belize, about three months later in early December. The focus would be on medicinal plants and spiritual healing, as well as women's health. My heart soared at the chance to learn about these other aspects of treatment that seemed to go beyond the scientific confines of my Western medical education—and to travel to Belize. Consciously, I knew I couldn't tolerate the jungle lifestyle Rosita had chosen, but a small adventurous part of me was excited that I could experience a little bit of Rosita's colorful story. I couldn't wait to sign up.

Rosita's fifteen-acre Belizean farm retreat, named after the goddess Ix Chel, was surrounded by rain forest. In *Sastun*, Don

Elijio explained, "Ix Chel is Lady Rainbow, and she is guardian of all the forest plants and queen of all forest spirits who guard the plants and animals. She is also a friend to the healer."

Rosita's house was on higher ground, with the guest cabins on the main level. The guest quarters were sparse but adequate. There were modern conveniences like electricity and running water. The bath and restroom facilities were communal, located in a different building. At night, the gravel pathways between structures were lit by small lamps placed fifteen inches above the ground, but flashlights were a must in order to maneuver in the dark.

We were welcomed by Rosita at dinner on the first evening. The students had arrived from different destinations during the early part of the day, and meeting during the evening meal ensured that everyone would be present for the orientation. The dining area where we ate and held our discussions was simple and had a jungle feel, with thatched roofs, dried palm strands, and sticks widely spaced to provide a division between the rooms. With picnic tables, these structures allowed fantastic views of the rain forest greenery during the day. During the evening gatherings, incense was burned to ward off the mosquitoes.

Rosita described the different sections of the farm where we were free to roam when not having lectures. The classes were to be held in a decent-sized gazebo on the way up to her house from the cabins. Treating rooms were close by and allowed hands-on training for the students. This clinical area was also where Rosita's patients were evaluated and treated.

The property was more manicured than I had envisioned. During the day, it looked like any other working farm. It was evident that the retreat center was self-contained. There were huge sections growing edible plants. Almost all the food was grown on the farm: papaya, chocolate beans, tomatoes, lettuce, kale, and amaranth, enough for the many guests passing through. There was also an area designated for medicinal plants and flowers, a live pharmacy present on the grounds, readily available year-round and fresh. There was no need to hunt for healing herbs.

Wandering away from the buildings in the main living area, the smell of humus, the mixture of humidity with the natural decaying matter of forest vegetation, became stronger. After morning class on the second day, I roamed to a medicine trail dedicated to Don Elijio Panti. It was created on the grounds of the farm to simulate the many walks that Rosita took with Don Elijio as he pointed out medicinal plants while gathering herbs.

Rosita was friendly and a good teacher, but was at home and definitely wanted her privacy. She was not available other than for scheduled classes and activities. She had her meals with her family and had a regular schedule of clinic patients, as well as duties on the farm. I respected her boundaries and decided to learn as much as I could and explore the Belizean farm that was part of our classroom.

As I walked on this path of jumbled vines and tree trunks with the crunch of vegetation under my feet, the Sunday magazine picture where I first saw Rosita came to life. The cacophony of different birds and rhythmic sounds from unidentified insects was no longer imagined. My nose scrunched at the funky smell that had to be the skunk root that healed skin rashes. Black orchids clutched onto the tree barks with their roots open to the humidity. They didn't need soil to hold on to moisture. An occasional butterfly flew around me. Looking closely at the tree trunks and thorny vines, I saw all manner of insects crawling up and down, busy finding food and making sure they had a safe place to live. The jungle was alive.

When a welcomed breeze blew by, the palm trees with their wide leaves seemed to wave at me and allowed the sunlight to peek through. I would soon be out of the cool shade.

The next day, I experienced one of the most enjoyable activities of the workshop. In the morning lecture, Rosita talked about the healing powers of flower water. When speaking about praying and collecting plants, she confided, "I imagine, no, I see fairies and elves jumping into the bag. I give thanks to the spirits of the plants, and I tell them that I have faith that they will help me make a healing bath." She continued, "Healing baths are used for cleansing, clearing energy and to facilitate healing. Human beings cannot do this work alone; we need spirits. We need beings of light to work with us, and they want to work with us."

We were to make our own herbal baths. We would have the run of the gardens. Our instruction was to choose nine plants or flowers for our mixture. The number we picked was not as important as saying nine prayers while we were collecting our ingredients. This ritual would help every drop of our lustral water absorb the healing energy of the universe.

"Numbers are like prayers and hold a vibration," Rosita explained before she let us loose on her farm. "In the Maya culture, nine is a sacred number. The number nine is where the spiritual manifests as the physical."

I frolicked in the vast, sunlit garden, thinking, *Nine plants. Nine prayers. Nine Maya spirits. Okay. Take it all in. Analyze later.* There were about fifteen of us scattered throughout the farm, walking through the gardens picking flowers that appealed to us. Although it was a fun task, I'm sure everyone, including myself, was serious about finding the perfect combination of ingredients. This water would have the healing energy of the universe.

I looked for a plant that would help me relax to get a more restful night's sleep. For the past three days since arriving in Belize, I'd had a headache. A good night's sleep is what most helped to ease it. The first flower that called to me was a plant with a five-to-eight-inch trumpet-shaped white flower with its face upturned toward the Sun. After picking eight more brightly colored flowers, I filled my bucket of flowers with water and went to find a spot in the sunshine. I set the intention of my nine prayers to the universe for my highest good. Oscar and Susan also used Florida flower water for cleansing prior to their healing work. As I poured the energized water over me, I thought this was my version of their perfumed Florida water.

After basking in the Sun for a while, I walked back to my cabin in a meditative mood. I needed to change into dry clothes. Most of the other participants were either still in the sunshine or had scattered elsewhere. The rest of the day was a free period for relaxation and contemplation. I took this time to find the name and properties of the first large flower I'd chosen.

The flower was in the genus *Datura*. If consumed, *Datura* could be poisonous and induce delirium with hallucinogenic effects. Because of the latter property, it was commonly used in love potions. *Datura* also had medicinal uses. The seeds could be used as an analgesic, anti-helminthic, and as anti-inflammatory medication. The juice of the fruit could be applied to the scalp to treat dandruff and falling hair.

Further, certain species of *Datura* contained belladonna alkaloids, which had anticholinergic effects that blocked involuntary muscle movements, like breathing. Did the spirit of the plant communicate to me unconsciously, to teach me that this plant could have the effects I requested?

I wasn't going to consume the plant, but I picked some more of the flowers to lay beside my pillow when I slept. I would see whether breathing in the aura of the plant would help me rest.

Later that day, as the Sun went down, a different energy developed as I walked in the forest surrounding the farm. It wasn't just the awakening of nocturnal animals. Senses other than vision became heightened. Every time a branch cracked, I turned to see if I might catch a glimpse of what had caused it. Imaginary eyes watched me through the shadows of the rustling foliage. I stepped cautiously in my surroundings. Was that a branch or a snake on the ground?

I thought of Miss Hortense, a local Belizean midwife who had been part of the morning workshop faculty that day. She was born into a family of midwives on both sides of her family. Rosita spoke of Miss Hortense's experience tending wombs and her valuable contribution to the abdominal massage technique; she was one of the instructors training us with hands-on abdominal massage. Her kind face with a friendly smile was surrounded by shoulder-length salt-and-pepper curls.

After Rosita described her process of gathering herbs and flowers, Miss Hortense, who had extensive knowledge of medicinal plants, spoke with a quiet confidence as she shared her process for collecting healing vegetation. "I collect plants after six o'clock when the plants wake up. I give a prayer of thanks and faith so the spirit of the plant follows us home to strengthen the healing. Ego doesn't heal. When I don't believe, I pray sayin' I believe, help my unbelief."

In this early evening jungle setting, my mind wandered and I looked around to see if I could see the plant allies, the elves and fairies that Rosita and Miss Hortense spoke about. In Belize, I believed in the presence of these helpers of nature.

In an early evening teaching session after dinner, Rosita talked about the structure of her prayers when doing healing work with plant medicine. She explained that it should start with an invocation. "'In the name of,' whomever you are calling on as your ally, such as God, spirit guides, etc. Then, state your intention. 'In order to heal.' Thirdly, express that you have faith in the healing power of the plant that you picked. Next, thank the spirit guides, the ancestors, or God for their blessing in aiding your efforts. Lastly, a closing statement should include that you give thanks in the name of your allies and any other statements you feel in your heart. You could be thankful that you are a vessel for helping people's suffering and that you are being supported in your endeavors."

One student raised her hand and stated, "What you're telling us about the structure of a prayer could be used as a formula with bad intentions to hex someone or cast a spell as well."

Rosita said, "Intention is very important. There are good and bad motives, good and bad allies, just as there are good and bad people."

In Belize, people believed that bad spells could be cast. Counterspells were then needed. Remediation rituals were prescribed. Behaviors were attributed to outside forces. There were good and evil *curanderos,* healers; not all of them had the best intentions.

In passing, Rosita mentioned that she believed her son had had a love spell cast on him and she knew what to do about it. I wondered, *How do you distinguish an infatuation spell from a fool in love?* And it piqued my curiosity that Rosita had a remedy.

It was almost comical, except that I wasn't privy to the whole story of what had occurred for her to believe her son was under such a spell. I'd experienced how grounded she was in her workshops, so I didn't discount her opinions.

Looking out the opened windows of our classroom, I noticed the darkening of the sky and the increasing sounds of the night creatures awakening. Cool breezes flowed inside but couldn't change the indoor temperature with the fifteen-plus warm students.

Nightfall triggered a metaphysical question by another student: "When casting out an evil spirit, where do they go?"

The well-being of the victim, the inhabited person, was considered to be more important than the disembodied entity. No more thought was given to the entity once exorcised. Out of sight, out of mind. I thought this was a practical question. I was interested in the answer.

Rosita answered the question by telling a story. "Ghosts mostly represent lost souls who died violent deaths, whose lives were cut short before they could psychically prepare. They can wander for years. Burn copal, tell them they are dead. Tell them the reality of what they're living is not the promise of the afterlife."

In Rosita's book *Sastun,* she explained that some remedies have dual purposes. For physical ailments, copal is used for upset stomach and intestinal parasites. For the spiritual conditions, it's effective in warding off evil spirits and spiritual disease, such as envy, fright, and grief.

She shared an experience. "I once stayed in a converted castle during one of my workshops in Europe. The proprietor told me the castle was beautiful but didn't have a comfortable atmosphere. In fact, it had a reputation of being haunted. Guests who stayed there would hear frightening sounds and describe feeling strangely about the place. They always seemed anxious to leave."

Rosita continued, "Ghosts like damp, dark corners—like in a castle. Ghosts will do all sorts of things to frighten people. They live on physical energy that they can suck from living things. Fear and anxiety are a heightened state of energy that they feed on. When you do this work, you cannot be emotionally upset. You cannot be drinking or taking drugs. This opens up bridges in your aura, leaving you vulnerable."

As a medical practitioner, I understood this concept. If a health-care worker gets caught in the emotion of situation, he or she becomes useless. To adequately heal, they have to be in control, acting in a rational and efficient manner.

Rosita told us that she'd asked the castle owner, "Was there something dramatic that happened here in the past?" He'd replied that there was a history of a violent death, but it was a long time ago and he didn't know the circumstances.

Walking around the castle after her conversation with the owner, she asked herself, *Where am I going to find healing herbs in this rocky place?* She started to pray to the Maya spirits. She called on her mentor, Don Elijio, to assist her efforts. Miraculously, she found rue, her plant ally, growing between cracks on the rocky grounds and she was able to prepare her purification water. In spiritual healing, rue wards off evil energy. It's also used to treat menstrual cramps.

Rosita picked a room in the castle where she felt a discordant energy. "It felt like a male," she said, speaking of the ghost. Additionally, she explained, "When there is an entity, I get a chill in my spine. The hair on my forearms stands up." She described that she felt a pull on her solar plexus, telling her the ghost was close.

Rosita called on the entity's mother to help her son. It didn't matter if the entity was the victim or the perpetrator of the violence. She then conversed with the energy inhabiting the castle, drawing him in. "Your mother is here waiting for you." Rosita explained that no matter how lost a personality might be, he or she always responded to their mother, the only person who loved them unconditionally. The mention of their mother had the ability to open any child's heart—no matter what age.

Slowly, in her mind's eye, Rosita described seeing a figure kneeling before her, signaling his consent to the ritual. He was ready to be sent on. She then called in the angels of light to join hands with his mother and surround the figure in a circle of loving support, making it hard for him to turn back from the light. Rosita continued the ceremony, sprinkling the lustral water made with rue around the presence.

Rosita described, "I felt a push and pull tugging at my solar plexus as the spirit hesitated. He was afraid to go." In closing, she emphasized, "This work is not easy. It took me three times to get him to go to the light."

During my week in Belize, I had experiences that wouldn't be easy to translate to treatment in the Western medicine that I practiced. The herbal baths in the sunshine with plants of my own choosing, collected with the use of prayers, was individualized for me. Sending a spirit to the light was not rote procedure. It took lustral water and prayers, as well as a capable facilitator.

I don't have any specific conclusions about some of the experiences I've had, only that anything is possible when the setting is right.

I was raised in the Catholic tradition where the weekly mass included a ceremony that transformed a wafer of bread and a chalice of wine into the body and blood of Christ. There was a stratum of different angels to call on. A generic guardian angel could be called upon to assist in any situation. Specific saints were beseeched to help in personal circumstances. St. Anthony is the patron saint of lost items whom I'd solicited for help many times. Faith seemed to be a common factor. Even in Western medicine, faith in the doctor and other health-care professionals contributed to healing, combined with medication.

There is a deep investment in preserving cultural legacy. There are people who work to preserve Indigenous knowledge so it's not lost with the passing of sages. Rosita wrote about her experiences with the revered medicine man Don Elijio Panti. She became his apprentice in order to preserve his healing wisdom. She'd traveled to disseminate and preserve Don Elijio's curative traditions. Don Oscar also facilitated workshops and pilgrimage tours to perpetuate the rituals and medicine practices of his Andean people.

In a sense, I saw myself as Iris's apprentice. Iris practiced a branch of knowledge with a lengthy history derived from ancient cultures. I learned the astrology she taught and put it to work by following and living the basic tenets of the subject. I felt the same motivation to disseminate my experiences as a testament to the utility of astrology.

All three used the visible part of nature in their work. Rosita and Oscar used plant medicine and prayer to communicate with the unseen spirit guardians of nature to facilitate the healing potential of the greenery. Iris used the extended nature of the sky inhabitants in her work. She put herself in an altered state to facilitate interpretation of the map of the sky. Her work also has the potential to heal by helping clients understand themselves.

Benevolent humanitarian traditions should survive as part of the culture's legacy from which future civilizations can learn. In one class, Iris had introduced a symbol of a mythical Sankofa bird from the Akan tribe in Ghana. It had its feet and body firmly planted forward with its head turned backward. In its mouth was an egg, symbolizing the future. The message of the Sankofa bird is that to move forward, we must look back to remember what we forgot. We must learn from the wisdom of the past to establish a strong future.

Chapter 20:

Star Gazer

In 2002, I quit my first two jobs and took a part-time clinical position at the local hospital, in addition to my administrative position. After two years, I quit the clinical position as well and decided to continue full-time work as an administrator. It allowed more flexibility, and when I took extended trips, I didn't feel guilty when leaving patients to the care of other colleagues.

Besides work and visiting my parents, I would go to an occasional Vedic astrology class. I also spent a fair amount of time exploring the Bay Area. I even became a docent at the California Academy of Sciences in San Francisco.

I kept in contact with Iris and got annual readings, but it was more like catching up with a dear friend and teacher. SAGE had not worked out for Susan. She moved from Miami to Prescott, Arizona, to do healing work, and she started leading international pilgrimage tours.

I hadn't been able to go to Susan's pilgrimage tours to sacred sites, but in 2009 she called to say she was organizing a tour to Peru. Did I want to come? Yes, I wanted to go back to the Andes and the people who worked with nature, who saw the Earth and the sky as a continuum of their environment. They had celebrations honoring the stars as places where their ancestors hailed from and where one day they could return.

Since my first visit to Peru in 1997, I had explored other forms of healing, such as my 2002 trip to Belize. In the interim, I'd done research about the history of the sacred Andean sites and the shamanic ceremonies led by Oscar and Susan. The structures like Machu Picchu were built in alignment with the natural environment. The rituals performed allowed connection with the ancestors in the nonphysical realm and with the star people who were inhabitants of the sky.

Like my interest in trying to find out how psychics, mediums, and tarot card readers got their information, I was curious too about the subtle energies in these sacred sites. Susan would help facilitate my query. She was comfortable with the unseen world.

What I was pursuing seemed like stuff from futuristic science fiction movies, but it seemed to be within reach. I was more informed about the circumstances that I'd be participating in and would be more than just a tourist taking in all the new sites like on the 1997 trip.

So, in September of 2009, I went to experience Peru again, not expecting anything in particular to happen but with the goal of being open to whatever experience might come to me.

Our two-week Peru pilgrimage didn't include the jungle symbolizing the underworld, the *Uku Pacha* in Andean cosmology. We explored *Kay Pacha*, the middle world where humans lived. Southwest of Lima, we flew over the Nazca Lines, the giant designs etched into the ground that could only be viewed from above. We then headed east to Cusco and spent a day in the city to acclimate a bit in the high altitude. We then descended by train to the isolated cloud forest of Peru where the Andes merges with the Amazon rain forest, from 9,160 feet to 7,972 feet to the main objective of our trip, Machu Picchu.

At these heights, we would explore the *Hanaq Pacha*, the upper world, the realm of gods, the spiritual realm of the three worlds in Andean cosmology.

As we alighted from the train station in Aguas Calientes, our group, easily targeted as tourists, was surrounded by local vendors with their snacks and souvenirs. A flute player demonstrated the flutes he'd made by playing the familiar tune of Simon and Garfunkel's "El Cóndor Pasa (If I Could)." When I first disembarked from the train on my 1997 trip and heard the melody, I mistakenly thought that the Peruvians copied the duo's tune. But in fact, it was the other way around; Simon and Garfunkel were inspired by the Andean folk melody. I was back in the Inca citadel of Machu Picchu.

There were only five in our group, so it was easy to get a consensus on our schedule of activities. Our guide gave us a tour of the major ritual sites on the first day, but the next three days we were free to explore the structures where we wanted to spend more time. I spent most of my time hiking around the buildings, visiting the major sites: the Temple of the Sun, the Temple of the Three Windows, and the Intihuatana Stone, also known as the Hitching Post of the Sun. Susan and I even hiked up to the Temple of the Moon on the mountain behind the citadel complex. I went by myself to many of the structures to see if I could feel any energies, but it was difficult to concentrate and meditate because of the many other tourists enjoying themselves and taking pictures at this UNESCO World Heritage Site with its meticulous green landscaping and fantastic vistas.

On my 1997 trip to Machu Picchu, *curandero* Oscar gave a metaphysical explanation of the structure of the funerary rock. It was a passageway to another realm, a way to connect with the star brothers, more commonly known as aliens. The rock was shaped with the same kitelike configuration of the Southern Cross constellation when connecting the points of the four brightest stars. At the latitude of 35 degrees south and all latitudes further south, the Southern Cross was circumpolar, meaning that it is continually visible above the horizon at any hour of the night all year around.

Oscar had described that during a funeral ceremony, the spirit of the deceased would be propelled through the portal formed by the constellation to unite with the star brethren. In life, meditation while lying on the stone platform could facilitate journeying to another dimension.

I came back several times during our three-day stay to lie on the rock and see if I could meditate my way through the gate of the Southern Cross, but I couldn't quiet my mind enough. Although the rock was cool, the heat of the Sun directly over me was uncomfortable and I couldn't spend as much time as I wanted in deference to the lines that had formed waiting for their time on the rock.

The architecture of Machu Picchu was built in alignment with the celestial bodies. I was trying to get a connection with the stars and the star brothers to see why I was drawn to the study of astrology. I couldn't feel any energy. No visions. No inkling of a connection. I just felt like a tourist.

On the second evening as our group met for dinner, Susan told us of another experiential opportunity. On the hotel grounds was a domed structure made of wood and thatch, about twelve feet in diameter, used for steam baths but which could function as a sweat lodge. Susan had a Native American background, and she wanted to take this opportunity to celebrate her tradition. Her grandmother was Cherokee and had encouraged her healing path. This sentiment went along with the Inca prophecy that the cultures of the Indigenous peoples of North and South America would come together for a common goal of preserving Mother Earth. She arranged the purification ceremony to start two hours after dinner. I wanted to participate, feeling open and curious about all the opportunities that were coming my way.

Five of us sat in the small, enclosed hut with the fire pit burning. Susan acquiesced as the elder of our group asked to chant the opening invocation. The prayer started with the invitation to all the beings of light present in the seen and unseen world to join us. She called in the plant and animal spirits and all our ancestors to come and participate in our celebration ceremony.

At first, the warmth was comfortable as the temperature outside had cooled to the low sixties with sundown. Then Susan started adding more fuel to the fire, as well as water to create steam. I positioned my face close to the ground to breathe the cooler air and to try to avoid inhaling the circulating ash. Drinking cool water didn't help me to be more comfortable.

A sweat lodge, also called a sweat, is a purifying ritual using intention, prayer, chanting, and intense heat to create an altered physical state. The heat causes dehydration and increased body temperature that could result in disorientation and reduced awareness of the environment, with the result of stimulating awareness and insight. Depending on the person's constitution, the stress of the sweat could also lead to rapid decline of all body systems, especially if the person wasn't aware of what was happening to his or her body and continued to stay in the heated environment.

With my face one inch from the wooden floor and Susan creating more steam, all I could think of was my discomfort. I alternated wiping the dripping sweat from my face and splashing it with drinking water. I was hot and getting more irritated than insightful. It wasn't worth it for me. After thirty minutes, I signaled that I was leaving.

I crawled out and sat in the walkway just outside the domed structure taking in the cool night air. After recovering, I took the long way back to my casita, watching how leaves on either side of the garden pathway reflected the light of the torches that directed me. As my gaze continued upward, the darkness blunted my depth perception, and the dot of lights overhead seemed to form a canopy that flowed from the ornamental plants.

When I got to my room, I slid one of the wooden armchairs outside, wrapped a blanket around me, and listened to the sounds of the night while staring at the stars in the sky. At home, I loved sitting outside and watching the night sky, and here there was minimal light pollution and the luminous bodies were so much brighter. The number of stars in the sky was infinite. That was how I got into an altered state that night.

I surveyed the celestial view above, contemplating nothing in particular. But then all of a sudden, I had a hit of déjà vu. I'd looked at this sky panorama before. I scanned my mind as to when. Ahh, okay, this was similar to the sweeping view of the night sky that the man in my dreams saw. He started coming to me when I was in my twenties and appeared in my dreams again when I was in my midthirties, just before my first trip to Peru in 1997. He walked continuously during the day with a sense of purpose I couldn't ascertain. He only stopped wandering to rest when the Sun went to sleep. And before he closed his eyes, he gazed at the lights in the sky, wondering. The night sky was my connection with Machu Picchu.

We had different physical forms, separated by time and space but united by a mutual connection through the vista of the stars. He had wanted me to see this view. I felt his sense of awe and curiosity at the vastness of the distant space above him. I felt an awareness that he may have stopped here. Then, I thought about the structures that I'd seen yesterday and knew he must've stopped here. He had found kindred spirits in the Incas. He found people who also looked at the points of light overhead and wondered. These people who built Machu Picchu observed that the movement of the wandering stars was aligned with the seasons of nature. They synchronized their lifestyle with this connection. The Earth and the sky environments were one. The celestial panorama was beyond their horizon, but it was still a part of their natural world.

As I sat in the cool evening air with a clear view of the lights in the sky, I was elated with my newfound knowledge. I felt that he found people of like mind here. I felt my connection with the man. The man and I were like long-lost cousins separated by space and time, who found the link through which we were connected, with people who lived in harmony with nature and the heavens.

I started imagining what this man's life would've been like in this community and comparing it to my life now. During the time of the Incas in Machu Picchu, this man might've been trained to be an astronomer, associating the cycles of the planets and stars with agrarian cycles. He might've participated in the architecture of the citadel. I felt this was where he stopped wandering. I felt that he stayed here and became part of this community.

As a woman in that lifetime, I don't think I would've attained such status in that society. I'm a different iteration of that man. For me, I don't belong here and my journey will continue. From here, I'm to propagate the story of the stars in my own way.

In my life now, as a woman, I've had more options. I gravitated toward the science of astronomy combined with the art of interpretation. I've studied how the planetary cycles affect people. My interest in the stars manifested in astrology.

Visiting different countries is akin to time travel. Airplanes are truly time machines. Even short tours into a different culture's lifestyle—eating what they eat, listening to their music, seeing their manner of dress, and participating in their sacred ceremonies—allows immersion into a world that previously would have been an experience I could only read about.

On my first trip to Peru twelve years earlier, the three weeks of continuous movement by airplane, bus, train, and boat to Lima, Cusco, Machu Picchu, and the Amazon region didn't allow much time for reflection. There was a lot of interaction within our group of twenty travelers. This trip had less distraction with only four other companions, allowing time for contemplation.

At the end of my 2009 Peru pilgrimage, I felt a sense of closure I didn't expect. I'd connected with the wandering man in my dreams on Machu Picchu, a place I recognized that he had been looking for. It had taken me twelve years to understand that he was an unconscious part of me. And now his journey was done. It was as if he'd passed the torch to me, acknowledging the path I had taken to find a link bridging terrestrial life with the celestial spheres in studying astrology. After this trip, he no longer appeared in my dreams.

Early one morning, Stacey, Iris's daughter, called me. It was May 15, 2017, and when I picked up the phone, she was crying. Iris had passed earlier that morning. I cried too. My friend and teacher had died. Iris had been the one who encouraged my thoughts of travel and adventure through the study of astrology.

I hadn't seen her since 2005. We had only talked on the phone once a year since then. But when I would hear her resonant voice, it reassured me that she was still strong. I'd last spoken to her two years earlier. We talked at length, and that was when she told me about her treatments for stomach cancer and then breast cancer after that.

I wanted to visit her, but she didn't want me to see her sick. She was strong-willed and I knew that if I flew to Florida without her permission, she wouldn't see me. She ended our call with her usual humor. She laughed and said, "If I had died at eighty-nine years old, I would've died healthy."

I hadn't been able to make the funeral because I was sick, but I traveled to Fort Lauderdale four weeks later and sat on Stacey's balcony. We reminisced about her mother while listening to a recording of her last radio interview. It was like being in one of Iris's weekly demonstrations. The Sun had set, but we didn't move. We continued talking past early evening.

During a pause in our conversation, Stacey turned and glanced behind her, past the kitchen, and asked, "Do you see something moving by the door? It's like a little cloud."

We hadn't turned on any lights inside. I looked behind me toward the entrance, fearful that I was going to see a ghost. Had the spirits forgotten my childhood request to come only in my sleep? I didn't want to see Iris's image, even if she was my friend in the earthly plane. "I don't see anything," I replied.

Stacey's focus returned to our conversation, but when I was getting ready to leave, I stopped in front of the refrigerator where Stacey had placed the last picture she'd taken of her mother. Holding my breath, I yelled, "Hey, Stacey, come here!"

Iris's picture had transformed. I'd seen the image the night before—of Iris in an elevator after they'd returned from one of her many medical appointments. The original picture already looked like an apparition, with the light in the elevator reflected on the wall behind her, making it look like a fuzzy Moon loomed over her head. Her chin-length hair was wavy white. She was smiling. With her protuberant eyes and dark sweater, Iris already looked ghostlike.

When she came, I said, "Stacey, look at this picture! Your mom was here!" The picture's rectangular edges were now outlined by rainbow colors that weren't present the night before. I knew because I had taken a picture of this photo as a last memento of my friend. Iris did come to visit us. Her presence must've been the cloud that was visible to Stacey when we were talking on her balcony.

When I first met her, photography was a serious hobby for me. Iris knew I would notice the photograph. I hugged Stacey in disbelief, but more to calm myself from the evidence that a spirit had visited us.

All Stacey said was, "I told you she was here."

Epilogue:

Curiosity Leads to Exploration

After returning to Oakland from my 2009 Peru trip, I got busy with my administrative duties but continued to look for information on astrology. Reading, going to classes, and listening to different podcasts and YouTube discussions gave me the perspective of the many traditions being practiced. I was convinced that there was truth to astrology, as it had survived thousands of years in different forms in many countries. I believed that astrology had practical utility in guiding aspects of life as defined by the twelve sections of life outlined in the horoscope, but I had to become more adept at the subject, even if it was just with my own chart.

The study of astrology had guided me well. It gave me another perspective to view myself beyond society's standards. I saw my strengths more objectively and was comfortable with choices I'd made to pursue my interests in learning and traveling. I was less anxious when my friends and family chided me for not settling down with a home and family, telling me that my biological clock was ticking. I deflected some of my colleagues' and friends' opinions that I was flaky for flying off to study with Indigenous healers and believing in astrology. They would tell me, "You're already a doctor. What more do you want?"

I pursued my curiosity to learn more about how people got information from nontraditional communication. I wanted to know about different types of healing techniques. My chart confirmed what I knew: with hard work, I could take care of myself and explore my ongoing interests.

Originally, I planned to write this book about my mentor and friend, Iris. She helped me see my potential in a unique way, through the astrological chart. I wanted to write about her influence and her gift of foresight, but when I put pen to paper, I realized I didn't know much about her personal life. Iris never wanted to get too emotionally involved with her clients or students because then it would be hard for her to give impartial consultations. She would only want to convey good news in her readings.

When I explained my dilemma to her, she told me, "Just write. It's going to change anyway." It did. I never thought that I would be writing about myself, but I had to write about what I knew: my journey of discovery. Many people go through the process of questioning their purpose in life. I want to share the map I found and how I got clarity by learning the astrological language of symbols.

As previously discussed, the message of the Sankofa bird is that to move forward, we must look back to remember what we forgot. We must learn from the wisdom of the past to establish a strong future. Astrology could be an adjunct method to study many aspects of life. All that is needed is birth data: date, time, and location. It does take effort to learn, but I believe that everyone has a map that can prepare them for their journey in life. The map doesn't solve all problems, but most questions can be clarified, if not answered.

My search for a handbook for life started in medical school as wishful thinking. The rigors of medical training made me wonder if being a physician was my path or if it was just a profession that I knew I could achieve. My circumstances and curiosity sowed the seeds for my search for an answer. With hard work, I finished training and moved to stages in life where I could, little by little, appreciate my education for what it allowed me to do as a physician, and also to seek a handbook for life. After medical school, my plan had been to be a clinical doctor the rest of my life, but after starting my search, I began to follow the path of a doctor who'd also be an explorer of sorts.

Throughout my research process, I resonated with the tenets of astrology. I found a map of my potential and got clarity and validation to pursue my passions to learn about different healing techniques and past cultures, and to travel. Over the years, I met people who had connections with the unseen world. I met Iris, who shared her knowledge and stoked my interest in astrology. I experienced how Indigenous healers utilized and preserved Earth's natural resources. I learned how ancient people combined their way of life with the movement of the stars. I learned from people who shared their knowledge on the Internet. The knowledge I gained helped to broaden my perspective on life. It showed me how limited the boundaries were that I had initially seen for myself. The world was so much larger with more opportunities than I imagined when I was eighteen.

The map, my horoscope, gave me validation to take the scenic route in life. Some of the roads were bumpy and almost caused me to turn back onto familiar roads that society deemed should be my path: work, marriage, and having children. But curiosity got the best of me, and I continued on a different path. I worked as a physician and during my free time I studied and participated in complementary medicinal techniques. I was scared at times, but I had faith that my map would lead me somewhere interesting, and that I would emerge wiser for my effort.

It was by word of mouth that I got introduced to Iris and Western astrology. I got a simple introduction to Chinese astrology in Chinese restaurants while reading the paper place-mats illustrating the different animals that represented certain years. I found out about Vedic astrology when given a book on the subject by a coworker. I learned on the Internet about the many different points of view growing out of different cultures and diverse schools of thought. But it was the Sun sign horoscopes in the newspaper next to the cartoon section that had initially sparked my interest. I wanted to know how astrology worked. It took years until I was able to pursue my curiosity, but now it has become a significant part of my life. I am sharing my experience because I feel that astrology can be helpful for any individual who wants to learn about themselves, whether they become a student of the subject or seek a professional for advice. I continue to be a student of astrology.

Tami Simon of Sounds True, Inc., which "offers transformational programs to help you live a more genuine, loving, and meaningful life," interviewed Rose Marcario, former CEO of Patagonia, a sustainable clothing company. Rose suggests, "Ask questions that are so big that only your life can answer them."

Open yourself to curiosity. It has the potential to take you places you can't even imagine. It did for me.

Acknowledgments

E ffective written storytelling is more difficult than the oral tradition, as it has to recreate events in an orderly fashion while evoking emotion and stirring the imagination, without the aid of the storyteller's vocal inflections, hand gestures, and eye contact to engage the reader. It was an art that I had to learn to write my story.

I started by taking writing classes from Book Passage Bookstore & Café in Corte Madera, California. When I moved from California to Las Vegas, Nevada, I found Henderson Writers Group and joined a critique group, which gave me my first lessons in critical feedback. I took all the comments in stride and just kept writing anecdotes that were significant to my astrology journey. I would then have an archive of events that I could sequence to form the scaffold of my story.

Then, I found the world of writing conferences. It was in Kauai, Hawaii, that I heard Brooke Warner speak about memoir. She was enthusiastic and gave grounded information about the process of writing and the publishing industry that gave me hope that I could become a published author. It wouldn't be easy, but I wasn't afraid of work. The next year I participated in Write Your Memoir in Six Months, a mentorship program with Brooke and

Linda Joy Myers, founder and president of the National Association of Memoir Writers. After twelve months of their coaching, I had a viable memoir that would undergo several rounds of editing. I eventually signed with She Writes Press, where Brooke is a publisher.

I thank my friends Tami Takahashi and astrologer Theresa Spear for reviewing my manuscript and giving me constructive feedback.

I thank my medical school guidance counselor, B. Rutledge, who guided me to the path of possibilities and independence at a crossroads in my life when I was faced with external obstacles, self-doubt, and indecision.

There are now many organizations that promote astrological education and research in person and online. I have to thank astrologer Rick Levine (www.stariq.com), who has shared many YouTube discussions on the theory, history, and practical uses of astrology with which I've resonated. Thanks to my many teachers, too numerous to name, including Indigenous healers Oscar Miro-Quesada and Susan Griffin. I recommend the following astrological organizations and websites for further exploration: Association for Astrological Networking, American College of Vedic Astrology, www.astrologydc.com, www.applied vedicastrology.com, www.billsinclair.com, www.komilla.com, www.dgoldsteinphd.com, International Society for Astrological Research (ISAR), www.jameskelleher.com, Arsha Jyotish (jyotish. com), The Astrology Podcast, Susan Miller's Astrology Zone, National Council for Geocosmic Research, www.ronniedreyer. com, www.opaastrology.org, www.parasharaconference.com, www.MarcBoney.com, www.AnneOrtelee.com, United Astrology Conference, www.vedicchart.com, www.vedictraditions.com, www.vedicsciences.com, and Kepler College based in Seattle, Washington.

There are many more teachers, institutions, and conferences that I have not yet experienced. EXPLORE!

About the Author

Alicia Blando trained and practiced in the medical specialty of physical medicine and rehabilitation. While working as a physician, she became interested in how Indigenous healers diagnosed and treated their patients without the technology present in modern medicine. This curiosity was supported by what she learned about herself through the study of astrology. As a Western physician who has followed the tenets of astrology in her life, she believes that the practice of astrology can function as an adjunct method to study many aspects of life, including the tendencies for certain disease processes. Alicia works as a medical consultant. She currently resides in Las Vegas, Nevada.

She can be reached at www.aliciablando.com.

Author photo © Sidney Oster

SELECTED TITLES FROM SHE WRITES PRESS

She Writes Press is an independent publishing
company founded to serve women writers everywhere.
Visit us at www.shewritespress.com.

Dog as My Doctor, Cat as My Nurse: An Animal Lover's Guide to a Healthy, Happy & Extraordinary Life by Carlyn Montes De Oca. $16.95, 978-1-63152-186-7. A groundbreaking look at how dogs and cats affect, enhance, and remedy human well-being.

The Doctor and The Stork: A Memoir of Modern Medical Babymaking by K.K. Goldberg. $16.95, 978-1-63152-830-9. A mother's compelling story of her post-IVF, high-risk pregnancy with twins—the very definition of a modern medical babymaking experience.

The Longest Mile: A Doctor, a Food Fight, and the Footrace that Rallied a Community Against Cancer by Christine Meyer, MD. $16.95, 978-1-63152-043-3. In a moment of desperation, after seeing too many patients and loved ones battle cancer, a doctor starts a running team—never dreaming what a positive impact it will have on her community.

The Vitamin Solution: Two Doctors Clear the Confusion about Vitamins and Your Health by Dr. Romy Block and Dr. Arielle Levitan. $17.95, 978-1-63152-014-3. Drs. Romy Block and Arielle Levitan cut through all of the conflicting data about vitamins to provide readers with a concise, medically sound approach to vitamin use as a means of feeling better and enhancing health.

Amazon Wisdom Keeper: A Psychologist's Memoir of Spiritual Awakening, Loraine Y. Van Tuyl, PhD. $16.95, 978-1-63152-316-8. Van Tuyl, a graduate psychology student and budding shamanic healer, is blindsided when she begins to experience startling visions, hear elusive drumming, and become aware of her inseverable, mystical ties to the Amazon rainforest of her native Suriname. Is she in the wrong field, or did her childhood dreams, imaginary guides, and premonitions somehow prepare her for these challenges?

Beyond Jesus: My Spiritual Odyssey by Patricia A. Pearce. $16.95, 978-1-63152-359-5. In the crucible of grief following a friend's death, Patricia Pearce resolved to open herself to hidden dimensions of her existence—not realizing her quest would cost her her vocation as a Presbyterian pastor, open her eyes to the radical implications of Jesus's message, and uncover what she believes is the key to our spiritual evolution.